The Hellenistic Age

The Hellenistic Age

PETER THONEMANN

OXFORD
UNIVERSITY PRESS

Great Clarendon Street, Oxford, OX2 6DP,
United Kingdom

Oxford University Press is a department of the University of Oxford.
It furthers the University's objective of excellence in research, scholarship,
and education by publishing worldwide. Oxford is a registered trade mark of
Oxford University Press in the UK and in certain other countries

First Edition published in 2016

Impression: 1

Published in the United States of America by Oxford University Press
198 Madison Avenue, New York, NY 10016, United States of America

British Library Cataloguing in Publication Data

Data available

Library of Congress Control Number: 2015949592

ISBN 978–0–19–875901–0

Printed in Great Britain by
Clays Ltd, St Ives plc

CONTENTS

PREFACE

The three centuries which followed the Macedonian conquest of Asia, from the death of Alexander the Great (323 BC) to the fall of the Ptolemaic kingdom of Egypt (30 BC), are perhaps the most thrilling of all periods of ancient history. In this short book I have tried to convey some of the richness and variety of Hellenistic civilization, from the Library and Museum of Alexandria to the wild Afghan colonial frontier. The story of the Greek adventure in the East is one of the great romances of human history, and I hope that this book will inspire some readers to explore it further. A few suggestions for further reading will be found at the end.

The Hellenistic world spanned a vast geographic area, from the western Mediterranean to the Hindu Kush, and readers may find it helpful to use the maps on pages xii–xiii for orientation.

LIST OF ILLUSTRATIONS

MAPS

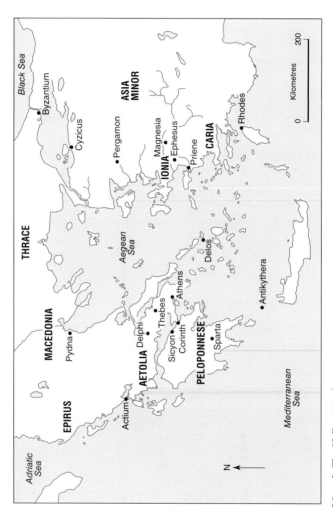

Map 1 The Hellenistic Aegean.

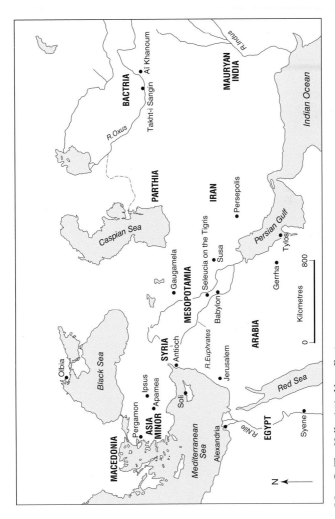

Map 2 The Hellenistic Near East.

philosophy at Aristotle's Lyceum. He visited Apollo's sanctuary at Delphi, where he carefully copied the god's oracular sayings ('Know thyself'; 'A friend's affairs are one's own'). He began to write, and he wrote about the strange new world starting to come into being: the religion of the Jews, Indian wisdom, the Persian Magi. Thanks to quotations preserved by later writers, we can still read a few fragments of Clearchus' lost philosophical works, *On Education*, *On Flattery*, *On Friendship* and others.

In the summer of 323 BC, Alexander, king of the world, died at Babylon. Within a few months, Alexander's empire had already begun to fracture into regional fiefdoms in the hands of hard-faced Macedonian generals: Ptolemy in Egypt, Antipater (and later Cassander) in Macedon, Perdiccas (and later Antigonus) in Asia. But for a young man of an inquisitive disposition, the world was opening up. Other young men of Soli had already made unimaginable lives for themselves in the Greek New World: Stasanor of Soli ruled as the governor ('satrap') of Drangiana in eastern Iran, and the sea-captain Hiero of Soli had explored the Arabian coast of the Red Sea as far as the Hormuz straits.

And so it was, in the first years of the third century BC, that the man from Soli set out for the East. All the lands from Syria to central Asia were now ruled by the greatest of Alexander's successors, King Seleucus I Nicator ('the Conqueror'). From the Syrian coast, Clearchus rode eastwards to the Euphrates; then downstream to the new Seleucid royal capital, Seleucia on the Tigris, a day's journey south of modern Baghdad. He crossed the Zagros mountains, and skirted the northern flank of the Iranian desert, on the long and dusty road to world's end: the great fortress of Aï Khanoum, on the banks of the River Oxus, in the far north-east of modern Afghanistan (described in Chapter 5).

Here, Clearchus found a little community of Greeks, building a new city beneath the snows of the Hindu Kush, 5,000 miles from Delphi. The city had a Greek theatre, and a Greek gymnasium; part of a lost work by Aristotle survives on a scrap of papyrus from the palace treasury at Aï Khanoum. Where Clearchus went next we can only guess: perhaps he crossed over the mountains into India, or maybe he set out on the long path back to the Mediterranean. But he left his mark on the stones of Aï Khanoum. In the tomb-complex of the city's founder, Kineas of Thessaly, Clearchus set up a limestone column bearing the sayings of the Seven Sages of Greece, which he had laboriously copied at Delphi thirty years earlier: 'As a child, be well-behaved; as a young man, self-controlled; in middle age, just; in old age, a good counsellor; in dying, without grief.' On the base of the column he had the following epigram inscribed:

> These wise sayings of famous men of old
> > Are consecrated in holy Pytho (Delphi).
> There Clearchus copied them carefully, and brought them
> > Here, to set them up, shining afar, in Kineas' precinct.

The stone survives today, a little battered by nomad invasions, but with the letters as crisp and clear as the day they were cut (see Figure 1). Since 2006 it has travelled even further than Clearchus did, as part of a roving worldwide exhibition of treasures from the Kabul Museum: it has been on show at the Musée Guimet in Paris, the British Museum

Figure 1 Clearchus of Soli at Aï Khanoum.

in London, and is due to spend 2016 on tour across Japan. If the museum guard looks the other way for long enough, you can run your finger across the name 'Clearchus', and reflect on a life less ordinary: beginning on the shores of Cyprus, and ending (perhaps) under the hard glare of a Bactrian sun. A Hellenistic life, if ever there was one.

A 'Hellenistic' Age?

Antiquity, the Middle Ages, the Early Modern period; Flavian Rome, Tudor England, *les trente glorieuses*; Archaic, Classical, Hellenistic. Historical 'periods' are blunt instruments, but without them we cannot talk about the past at all. Ancient Greek history is today conventionally divided into four periods: Archaic (from around 800 to 500 BC), Classical (500 to 323 BC), Hellenistic (323 to 30 BC) and Roman Imperial (30 BC to—say—AD 284). Hellenistic history, thus arbitrarily defined, is the subject of this book.

Like most epochs in ancient history (the 'Iron Age', the 'fifth century BC', 'Late Antiquity'), the idea of the 'Hellenistic' is a modern invention. The word itself is ultimately descended from a passage in the Biblical Acts of the Apostles, where the Jewish followers of Jesus are divided into *hellenistai* and *hebraioi*, terms which probably refer simply to their spoken language of choice (Greek or Hebrew). Early Modern Biblical scholars believed that the Jewish *hellenistai* used a special Greek dialect, the 'Hellenistic tongue' (*lingua hellenistica*), reflected in the Greek of the New Testament and the Septuagint.

The German scholar Johann Gustav Droysen (1808–84) was the first to use the term 'Hellenistic' not just of a dialect of the Greek language, but of a whole epoch in Mediterranean civilization, beginning with the Asiatic conquests of Alexander the Great in the late fourth century BC (334–323 BC). At the time of Alexander's conquests, wrote Droysen:

> East and West were ripe for fusion (*Verschmelzung*), and on both sides fermentation and transformation quickly followed. The new awakening of popular life led to ever more novel developments in the state and the intellectual sphere, in commerce and art, in religion and morality. Let us describe this new world-historical principle with the word 'Hellenistic'. Greek culture, in dominating the life of the world of the East, also fertilised it, and so created that Hellenism in which the paganism of Asia and Greece—indeed all antiquity itself—was destined to culminate.

For Droysen, the ultimate result of this cross-breeding between East and West was Christianity itself. Alexander's conquest of the East, and indeed the whole history of the Hellenistic world, was to culminate in the Christian faith, a quintessentially 'Hellenistic' religion born out of the fusion of the Greek and Oriental spirit. Happily, not all of Droysen's work was infected with this sort of nebulous mysticism: his enormous, unfinished *History of Hellenism* (1836–43) is, for the most part, a rather sober political history of the century from 323 to 222 BC.

For better or worse, Droysen's terminology caught on. Today, the word 'Hellenistic' is used to refer both to a historical epoch (the Hellenistic period) and to a geographical region (the Hellenistic world). It is also used of a whole range of cultural phenomena seen as characteristic of this region and period, such as Hellenistic kingdoms, Hellenistic poetry, Hellenistic sculpture, Hellenistic religion and so on.

The Hellenistic world, as usually understood, was a relatively narrow temperate zone of western Afro-Eurasia between the 25th and 45th parallels, stretching from the Adriatic and Libya in the west to the Himalayas in the east—broadly speaking, the lands ruled by Alexander the Great at his death in 323 BC. This zone includes the whole of the eastern Mediterranean and the Black Sea, Egypt and the Levant, Mesopotamia, the Iranian plateau, and the lands immediately to the north and south of the Hindu Kush. From the fourth to the first century BC, all of these regions were either Greek-speaking or ruled by Greek-speaking dynasties. Historians sometimes refer to Hellenistic Carthage, Hellenistic Arabi, or even Hellenistic India, in order to highlight the cultural connections between those outlying regions and the 'core' Hellenistic world; but most people would find something perverse about the notion of, say, Hellenistic Ireland or Hellenistic China.

Most modern histories of the Hellenistic period begin in 323 BC, with the death of Alexander the Great, and finish in 30 BC, with Octavian's incorporation of Ptolemaic Egypt into the Roman empire. The starting point is obvious enough. Alexander's swift, violent, and dramatic conquest of the Achaemenid Persian empire between 334 and 323 BC was a geopolitical event of the first significance, establishing Macedonian rule across vast stretches of western Asia. The 'globalization' of Greek culture in the wake of Alexander's conquests is perhaps the best argument for separating off a 'Hellenistic' Age from earlier periods of Greek history.

Things are much less clear-cut at the lower end of the period. The major Macedonian successor kingdoms in Europe, Africa, and Asia eventually collapsed in the face of Roman expansion in the west and Parthian expansion in the east, but the process was drawn-out and uneven. Macedon itself became a Roman province as early as 146 BC, but the Ptolemaic dynasty of Egypt lasted until 30 BC, and some small Hellenistic states (such as the Bosporan kingdom of the eastern Crimea) survived deep into the Roman Imperial period. As a result, the modern historiography of the later Hellenistic period is, frankly, a bit of a mess. Macedon after 146 BC is usually treated as part of Roman history, even though in most respects 'early Roman Macedonia' had far more in common with the late Hellenistic kingdoms in Asia than it did with, say, Roman Spain.

'Hellenistic culture' is, as we would expect, the fuzziest category of all. Here Droysen's idea of 'fusion' (*Verschmelzung*) still exercises a spectral influence. The Hellenistic period certainly saw large-scale migrations of Greek-speaking peoples into Egypt and Asia, and the Greek language, Greek lifestyles, and the institutions of the Greek city-state were widely diffused in the non-Greek lands conquered by Alexander. But whether we should see eastern Hellenism as marked by cultural fusion between Greeks and non-Greeks or, instead, by colonialism and apartheid, remains a hotly debated question.

Can we speak of a 'unified' Hellenistic world? The Seleucid, Antigonid, Ptolemaic, and Attalid monarchies really did have almost any criterion, we know far more about Hellenistic history than we do about the Archaic or Classical Greek world.

It is true that we are not well supplied with ancient narrative histories of the Hellenistic kingdoms. The break-up of Alexander's empire between 323 and 302 BC is recounted in Books 18–20 of Diodorus Siculus' *Library of History* (compiled *c.* 60–30 BC), supplemented by several early Hellenistic *Lives* by the biographer Plutarch (*c.* AD 45–120). Rome's rise to world power between 220 and 145 BC was described in the massive forty-book history of Polybius of Megalopolis (*c.* 200–118 BC). Only Polybius' first five books survive intact, but many of the missing portions can be reconstructed from Books 31–45 of Livy's *History of Rome*, which drew heavily on Polybius' lost narrative. The history of the Jewish people in the Hellenistic period is known in rich and circumstantial detail: I and II Maccabees (part of the Biblical *Apocrypha*) give a gripping contemporary narrative of the Jewish revolt against Seleucid rule in the 160s BC, and Books 11–12 of Josephus' *Jewish Antiquities* (first century AD) are a mine of information on Hellenistic Judaism.

The biggest gap in our knowledge is the political and military history of the third century BC, for which no reliable continuous account survives. Much of the 'core' narrative history of the third century is still deeply obscure: there may or may not have been a 'War of the Syrian Succession' between Antiochus I and Ptolemy II in 280/279 BC; we do not know whether the battle of Cos took place in 262 or 255 BC; and pretty much all that we can say about the Seleucid loss of southern Iran is that it must have happened some time between 280 BC and the early second century.

But narrative history is not everything, and the Hellenistic historian is amply compensated by an amazing wealth of documentary evidence of all kinds. The sands of Ptolemaic Egypt have preserved tens of thousands of bureaucratic and literary papyri, revealing the internal workings of the Ptolemaic state to a level of detail unimaginable for any earlier Mediterranean society. A single junior Ptolemaic financial official of the mid-third century BC, Zeno of Caunus, has left us an immense archive of more than 2,000 business documents, mostly relating to the management of a large private estate in the Fayyum oasis, south of modern Cairo. Papyri also offer us intimate access to the daily lives and mentalities of ordinary people in the Ptolemaic kingdom. We can read private letters, divorce-contracts, school exercises, and even the quirky dream-diaries of a Greek recluse and two little Egyptian twin girls in the temple of Serapis at Memphis:

> The dream that the girl Thaues, one of a twin, saw on the 17th of the month Pachon. I seemed in my dream to be walking down the street, counting nine houses. I wanted to turn back. I said, 'All this is at most nine.' They say, 'Well, you are free to go.' I said, 'It is too late for me.'
>
> The dream that Ptolemaios saw at the Moon Festival on the 25th of the month Pachon. I seem to see Thaues singing aloud in a rather sweet voice and in good spirits; and I see Taous laughing, and her foot is big and clean.

With rare exceptions, the papyri bear only on the internal history of Ptolemaic Egypt. Elsewhere in the Hellenistic world, our richest documentary evidence comes in the form of countless thousands of Greek inscriptions on stone. Hellenistic cities were a hubbub of public and private inscriptions, many of them running to hundreds of lines of vivid and intricate prose: inter-state treaties, honours for great civic benefactors, letters from Hellenistic kings; land-sales, temple-inventories, disputed wills, and accounts of divine epiphanies. An inscription from Pergamon in north-west Turkey, 237 lines long, describes in meticulous detail the duties of the city's *astynomoi*, the officials responsible for the upkeep of roads, fountains, cisterns, toilets and other public works. From the small city of Magnesia on the Maeander comes a dossier of more than sixty letters and decrees from Hellenistic kings and cities, recognizing the inviolability of the city and its territory. In many cases, these are the only surviving public documents from the cities concerned, making the Magnesian dossier a treasure-trove of evidence for Greek civic institutions from the Adriatic to the Persian Gulf.

Inscriptions often shed new light on major historical events. As Plutarch tells us in three curt sentences of his *Life of Demetrius* (written in the late first century AD), the year 287 BC saw a successful Athenian uprising against the rule of King Demetrius the Besieger (whose career is sketched in Chapter 3). In 1971, archaeologists working in the Athenian Agora uncovered a long honorific decree for a certain Callias of Sphettus, the commander of a Ptolemaic mercenary force in the Aegean. The inscription describes the course of the Athenian revolution in rich and moving detail, beginning as follows:

> When the revolution of the People took place against those occupying the city, they drove out the enemy soldiers from

the urban centre; but the fort on the Mouseion hill was still occupied, the countryside was in a state of war at the hands of the troops stationed in Piraeus, and Demetrius was marching from the Peloponnese with his army against the city. Callias, learning of the danger to the city, selected a thousand of the mercenaries stationed with him on Andros, paying their wages and providing grain-rations, and came at once to the city to help the People, acting in accordance with the good-will of King Ptolemy towards the people; and he marched his troops into the countryside and made every effort to protect the grain-harvest, so that as much food as possible could be brought into the city ... (etc.)

Only thanks to this text do we know that the Athenian rebels were backed by King Ptolemy I Soter (reigned 305–282 BC), Demetrius' chief rival for power in the Aegean basin. The inscription for Callias is now the cornerstone of our understanding of Ptolemaic foreign policy in the 280s BC.

Alongside written texts, the Hellenistic historian also has a terrific range of material evidence to draw on. Dozens of Hellenistic cities, sanctuaries, and fortresses have been excavated, from Greece to Afghanistan, among them the extraordinary Greek city of Priene, described in Chapter 6. The formidable site of Heraclea under Latmus in south-west Turkey preserves its entire Hellenistic wall-circuit all but intact, complete with towers, wallwalks and guardhouses (see Figure 2). Some of our best surviving examples of Hellenistic architecture come from Jordan: the fortress of Qasr il Abd near modern Amman (described by the Jewish historian Josephus) is a Hellenistic palace in miniature, and the city of Petra, capital of the Nabataean kingdom, gives us

Figure 2 The Hellenistic fortifications of Heraclea under Latmus.

a wonderful sense of the baroque cityscape of a late Hellenistic royal capital.

The study of gold, silver and bronze coins is more central to Hellenistic history than to any other period of antiquity. Several major Hellenistic states—most notably the Bactrian kingdom of central Asia and the Indo-Greek kingdoms of the Punjab—are effectively known to us only through their coin-issues. Coins also illuminate unexpected cultural and economic connections between far-flung parts of the Hellenistic world. In the third and second centuries BC, the Celtic peoples of north-west Europe struck coins for the first time; almost all of these coinages imitate the gold

Figure 3 A gold coin of Philip II of Macedon, minted *c.* 340-328 BC, and a Celtic imitation struck in Northern France or Belgium, *c.* 150-100 BC (images not to scale).

coins of Philip II of Macedon (359–336 BC), reflecting the extensive use of Celtic mercenaries by the major Hellenistic kingdoms (see Figure 3).

Finally, although contemporary narrative histories are thin on the ground, the Hellenistic states have left us a wonderful body of literary and scientific texts (the subject of Chapter 4). In the field of poetry, the *Mimiambs* of Herodas and some of the *Idylls* of Theocritus offer vivid sketches of daily life in the Hellenistic world; the *Exagoge* of Exekiel the Tragedian translates the Biblical narrative of Moses' flight from Egypt into the language and form of Greek tragic drama. We have a startlingly rich corpus of Hellenistic mathematical texts, including major works by Archimedes, Euclid, and Apollonius of Perge. At the interface between poetry and science stand 'didactic' poems such as Aratus' *Phaenomena* (on the constellations) and Nicander's *Theriaca* and *Alexipharmaca* (on venomous animals and poisons). New finds continue to enrich our knowledge of Hellenistic literature: 2001 saw the publication of a papyrus containing more than a hundred new epigrams by the third-century poet Posidippus.

As will be clear from the preceding pages, the Hellenistic historian has a rich and varied tapestry of sources to work from. One incidental result of this is that Hellenistic history is fun to write, and fun to read. Since 'straight' narrative history is usually impossible, we have to use our imagination. Ancient-history writing has few brighter jewels to show than Arnaldo Momigliano's *Alien Wisdom* (1975), Elias Bickerman's *The Jews in the Greek Age* (1988) or John Ma's *Antiochos III and the Cities of Western Asia Minor* (1999). William Tarn is not a fashionable writer nowadays—too Victorian, too moralizing, unsound on imperialism—but the incomparable opening pages of his *Antigonos Gonatas* (1913) still capture some of the excitement of Hellenistic history:

No part of Greek history should come home to us like the third century BC. It is the only period that we can in the least compare with our own; indeed, in some ways it is quite startlingly modern. We meet with half the things that we ourselves do, half the problems that we ourselves know. The days of Salamis and Sophokles are as remote from the men of that time as the days of Shakespeare or the Spanish Armada from ourselves. All the horizons have widened and opened out; civilization pulsates with new life, and an eager desire to try all things. Almost all the barriers are already down . . . And there is so much to be done; nothing less than the conquest, material, social, intellectual, of a whole new world.

This new world, in all its kaleidoscopic variety, is the subject of this book.

From Alexander to Augustus

Through his conquest of Achaemenid Persia, Alexander the Great created a single Macedonian empire stretching from the lower Danube and lower Nile in the west to the upper Indus and Oxus valleys in the east. In the first generation after Alexander's death (323–281 BC), this empire fractured into three successor kingdoms, each ruled by a Macedonian king: the Antigonids in Macedon, the Ptolemies in Egypt, and the Seleucids in western and central Asia. The history of the great successor states, their relations with the free Greek cities of the Aegean, and their eventual collapse in the face of Roman imperialism (and, to a lesser extent, Parthian expansion in Mesopotamia and Iran) is, without doubt, a tangled and confusing story. But it is also a thrilling one, as gripping in its unexpected reversals of fortune as any other period of ancient history. For sheer *Boys' Own* drama, there is little to match Aratus' night-time commando raid on Corinth in 243 BC (brilliantly narrated by Plutarch in his

Life of Aratus); for tragedy, little to compare with the fall and rise and fall of Demetrius the Besieger, or Cleopatra's long struggle to preserve her kingdom from Roman annexation. This chapter provides a road map to the twists and turns of Hellenistic history, from the accession of Alexander (336 BC) to the death of Cleopatra and the end of the Ptolemaic kingdom (30 BC).

Alexander the Great, 336–323 BC

In the 350s and 340s BC, Philip II of Macedon (reigned 359–336 BC) had transformed the Macedonian state from a small and backward kingdom on the northern fringe of the Greek world into one of the great powers of the Mediterranean. In the central Balkan highlands, Macedonian governors or vassal kings ruled over all the lands between the Adriatic and the Black Sea (Epirus, Illyria, Thrace). By 338, when Philip crushed an Athenian and Theban army at the battle of Chaeronea, most of mainland Greece had come under informal Macedonian dominance, with the Greek city-states of the south bound to Philip by unequal and humiliating alliances. Philip had made himself, in the words of his Athenian admirer Isocrates, 'the greatest of the kings of Europe'.

By the time of his mysterious assassination in October 336 BC, Philip II had already set his sights on the riches of the Persian empire to the east. We do not know the scale of Philip's Asiatic plans but, safe to say, his son Alexander exceeded them. In 334 BC, an army of Macedonians and Greek allies crossed into Asia. The Persian satrapies

In spring 327, the army marched on beyond the bounds of the former Persian empire, into India. Alexander's conquest of the Punjab and the Indus valley is a depressing and monotonous tale of carnage. The Macedonians established no lasting *modus vivendi* with the native population, and within two decades of Alexander's death, the Indian provinces were lost for good. But the invasion had far-reaching consequences. With the small principalities of north-west India fatally weakened by the Macedonians, an energetic Indian ruler, Chandragupta Maurya (reigned *c.* 317–293 BC), was able to unite the whole northern part of the subcontinent under his rule. The third-century empire of the Mauryas, stretching from Kandahar to Bengal, would be Alexander's chief legacy in the Far East.

By late 325 BC, the Macedonian army—thinned by a disastrous crossing of the Gedrosian desert (south-western Pakistan)—was back in western Iran, and the new masters of the world paused to draw breath. Aside from small pockets of local resistance, the entire Persian empire was now under Macedonian control. But after a decade of warfare, the Macedonian army was in desperate need of fresh blood. In autumn 324 BC, Alexander sent 10,000 Macedonian veterans, the greater part of the infantry army, off on their way back home under the command of his general Craterus, to be replaced by fresh levies from Macedonia. The king himself also began to take thought for his own eventual succession. In 328 BC, he had married Roxane, the daughter of a Bactrian noble, and in 324, after his return from the East, he also wed two women from the old Persian royal house, Stateira (daughter of Darius III) and Parysatis (sister of Darius' predecessor, Artaxerxes IV). At least one of these three women, Roxane, was pregnant at the time of Alexander's sudden death at Babylon on 11 June 323 BC.

Contemporaries wondered at the revolution in world affairs brought about by Alexander's conquest. In the early third century BC, the Athenian orator and statesman Demetrius of Phalerum reflected on the cruelty of Fortune:

> Do you think that fifty years ago, if one of the gods had foretold the future to the Persians or their king, or the Macedonians or their king, they would ever have believed what was to come? For in our own day not even the very name of the Persians survives, they who were formerly despots of the whole inhabited world, while the Macedonians, who previously were almost nameless, are now masters of all.

If there was ever a turning point in world history, the Macedonian conquest of Asia was it. Alexander 'the Great', indeed.

The Age of the Successors, 323–281 BC

Unrivalled as a conqueror, Alexander showed little interest in government. At his death in 323 BC, the Macedonian 'state' in Asia consisted of little more than Alexander's vast, battle-hardened army and a cadre of tough and ambitious Macedonian generals. The provincial bureaucracy, such as it was, consisted of whatever was left over from the old Persian system. This was, thus far, a Macedonian empire in name alone. But Alexander did leave behind him financial resources on a stupendous scale. In the last two years of his life, Alexander had begun to strike the vast gold and silver reserves of the Persian kings into coin, in order to pay off his veteran troops—who, quite reasonably, expected to share in the profits of conquest. A weak central state, an under-employed army, independent-minded generals, unlimited supplies of Persian silver, and, crucially, no capable adult successor to the dead king: the combination was an explosive one.

In the days after Alexander's death, the Macedonians at Babylon cobbled together a hasty compromise, by which Alexander's mentally defective half-brother Arrhidaeus would inherit the throne, along with Alexander's unborn baby by Roxane (if the child turned out to be a boy). One of the leading Macedonian generals, Perdiccas, would act as 'guardian' to the kings. But Perdiccas' rise to supremacy was really little more than a stroke of chance. Two other men, Antipater, Alexander's regent in Macedon, and Craterus, commanding a formidable force of 10,000 Macedonian veterans on their way back home to Europe, had claims at least as strong as his. The more prudent among Alexander's companions installed themselves in one or other of the rich western satrapies (Ptolemy in Egypt, Lysimachus in Thrace), and prepared for an uncertain future.

War broke out in 321. Ptolemy made the first move, seizing Alexander's body on its journey back to Macedon (an indication of his ambitions for his new Egyptian realm); Perdiccas' attempted invasion of Egypt ended in his ignominious death, assassinated by his own lieutenants. Craterus died in battle at around the same time, fighting Perdiccan forces in northern Asia Minor. At the conference of Triparadeisus in summer 320 BC, the Macedonians made one last attempt to hold the crumbling empire together. Antipater was appointed as guardian of the two kings, Arrhidaeus and Alexander IV (Roxane's son, by now a sturdy toddler), who returned with Antipater to Macedon. Ptolemy was left in control of Egypt (not that Antipater was given any choice in the matter). A flinty Macedonian officer, Antigonus the One-Eyed, already in his sixties, was appointed as 'general of Asia'. Although Antigonus' remit was initially limited to hunting down the remnants of Perdiccas' faction in Asia (particularly Craterus' killer, the rogue general Eumenes of Cardia), in practice his appointment hastened the division of the Asiatic and European parts of Alexander's empire.

Over the following two decades, five separate 'successor' states gradually took shape in the ruins of the Macedonian empire. In Egypt, Ptolemy ruled unchallenged, building a strong and coherent state around his capital at Alexandria (founded by Alexander himself in 331 BC). In Macedon, Antipater's son Cassander eventually emerged as the dominant figure. The two puppet kings did not encumber him for long: Arrhidaeus had been murdered in 317, and Cassander himself did away with Alexander IV in (probably) 310 BC. Thrace was ruled by the leonine Lysimachus, like Ptolemy a charismatic veteran of Alexander's campaigns. In Asia, a minor Macedonian officer called Seleucus, appointed as satrap of Babylon in 320 BC, gradually built up a formidable realm in Mesopotamia, Iran and the East; by 301 BC, he had established his rule over the entire eastern half of the old Persian empire.

Most powerful of all was Antigonus. With his son Demetrius the Besieger (Chapter 3), he built a rich and populous kingdom in western Asia, stretching from the Aegean to the Euphrates. And a 'kingdom' it now was: in 306, he and Demetrius became the first of Alexander's successors to assume the title of king, an act of potent symbolism that was swiftly imitated by their rival dynasts. To the cities of mainland Greece and Asia Minor, Antigonus and Demetrius presented themselves as the champions of Greek freedom and autonomy. No doubt this was a cynical move directed against Cassander, who had a notorious preference for authoritarian client-regimes in the Greek cities under his control. But Antigonus' ostentatious friendship towards the Greeks ('philhellenism') set the tone for the entire Hellenistic period. For the next three centuries, Hellenistic kings of all stamps strove to outdo one another in competitive generosity towards the Greek cities of the Aegean.

In 301 BC, the combined forces of Cassander, Lysimachus, and Seleucus routed the Antigonid royal army at the battle of Ipsus in central Turkey. By evening, the 81-year-old Antigonus the One-Eyed lay dead on the battlefield, and five kingdoms had become four. Demetrius—still only in his mid-thirties—fled with a few thousand men, and reigned for six years as a king without a kingdom. But the wheel of fortune turned: Cassander died in 297, and a civil war between Cassander's two sons in 294 gave Demetrius the opportunity to seize the throne of Macedon for himself. He lost it again to Lysimachus a mere seven years later, but by 276 Demetrius' son Antigonus Gonatas had recovered his father's kingdom. Demetrius' descendants (the 'Antigonids') would go on to rule in Macedon for the next century.

In the wake of the battle of Ipsus, Antigonus the One-Eyed's great kingdom in western Asia had been carved up between Lysimachus and Seleucus. In 281 BC Seleucus struck at Lysimachus' territories in Asia Minor; Lysimachus was killed at the battle of Corupedium, and four kingdoms became three. Ptolemy had died peacefully in his bed the previous year (succeeded by his son, Ptolemy II Philadelphus), leaving Seleucus as the last surviving contemporary of Alexander. In September 281, Seleucus crossed back over the Hellespont into Europe, fifty-three years after he had first crossed to Asia as a young man in Alexander's army. For a brief moment it seemed as though he might go on to seize Macedonia as well, thus reuniting Alexander's European and Asiatic realms for the first time in forty years. But no: Seleucus was assassinated by a pretender from the Ptolemaic royal house, and the moment passed. Not until the coming of Rome would Macedon and Asia again be reunited under a single ruler.

The Hellenistic Kingdoms, 281–220 BC

By the middle years of the third century BC, the new balance of power was firmly established. The bulk of Alexander's empire was divided into three Macedonian successor-states: the Antigonid kingdom in Macedon, the Ptolemaic kingdom of Egypt, and the vast Seleucid realm in western and central Asia.

By far the largest of the early Hellenistic kingdoms was that of the Seleucids in Asia. At the death of King Seleucus I Nicator, 'the Conqueror' (281 BC), the Seleucid realm covered the greater part of the former Persian empire, from Thrace (modern Bulgaria) to the borders with India, with a population of perhaps 25–30 million. In most parts of the kingdom, a tiny settler minority of Greeks and Macedonians ruled over multitudes of non-Greeks: Iranians, Babylonians, Arabs and the rest were excluded from all but the lowest rungs of the Seleucid administrative hierarchy.

It is easy to deplore the 'colonial' nature of Seleucid Asia, and modern historians have often taken a dim view of the Seleucid state more generally: weak, despotic, inefficient, and doomed to collapse. In 1938, William Tarn drew a famous contrast between the Seleucid kingdom and the Roman empire. 'The latter', he claimed, 'resembled a verte-brate animal':

> It expanded outwards from a solid core, the city of Rome. The Seleucid empire resembled rather a crustacean, not growing from any solid core but encased in an outer shell; the empire was a framework which covered a multitude of peoples and languages and cities. What there really was to an empire, officially, was a king, an army, and a bureaucracy—the governing and taxing officials in the several satrapies. It had no imperial citizenship, as the Roman empire had . . . What actually held the empire together was the personality of the quasi-divine monarch.

That understates the sensitivity and flexibility of Seleucid colonial rule. Like their Achaemenid Persian predecessors, the third-century Seleucid kings spoke to their dizzying range of subjects in a variety of local idioms. A building inscription in cuneiform Akkadian from the Babylonian sanctuary of Borsippa shows King Antiochus I Soter

(281–261 BC) proclaiming his devotion to a Babylonian deity, 'Prince Nabû, son of Esangila, first-born of Marduk, noble child of Erua'. A newly published Seleucid royal letter in Greek from eastern Iran shows King Seleucus II Callinicus (246–225 BC) ostentatiously defending the rights of the horse-rearing marsh-villagers of Helmand. The Seleucid kings were not just foreign conquerors. Indeed, one of the most imaginative and far-reaching strategies of the early Seleucid monarchs was the creation of an artificial new Seleucid 'homeland' in northern Syria: local towns and rivers were renamed after places in far-off Macedonia, and four splendid new cities were founded in the name of Seleucus himself (Seleucia in Pieria), his son Antiochus (Antioch by Daphne), his mother Laodice (Laodicea by the Sea) and his Iranian wife Apame (Apamea on the Orontes). Greek and Roman authors regularly referred to the Seleucid monarchs as 'Syrian kings', indicating the depth of the roots that the Macedonians eventually put down in Asia.

Nonetheless, by the mid-third century BC, the outer reaches of the Seleucid kingdom were already beginning to crumble. In the Far East, the Seleucid governor of Bactria (the modern Oxus valley, in northern Afghanistan) staged a successful revolt around 245 BC, and Seleucid north-east Iran was overrun only a few years later by a group of central Asian nomads (the Parni, better known as the Parthians). In the west, large parts of the Asia Minor peninsula (modern western Turkey) gradually came under the control of local dynasts (the Attalids of Pergamon, the Ariarathids of Cappadocia, and the royal houses of Bithynia and Pontus), all of whom seem to have won independence from the Seleucids by the later third century. This Balkanization of the Seleucid periphery was only briefly reversed by the campaigns of reconquest undertaken by the energetic Antiochus III (222–187 BC). By the early second century BC, much of Seleucus I's great Asiatic kingdom had broken up into a babble of regional principalities, leaving a relatively culturally homogeneous Seleucid 'core' in Syria and Mesopotamia.

The Ptolemaic kingdom of Egypt was very different. Like the Seleucids, the Ptolemies ruled over an ethnically mixed society, but here there were, to all intents and purposes, only two cultural groups concerned: the Graeco-Macedonian settler class (some 10 per cent of the total population), and the native Egyptians (perhaps 3.5–4 million in number). Ptolemy I Soter and his descendants ruled as traditional Pharaohs, preserving most of the traditional institutions of pharaonic Egypt (temples and priesthoods, regional government, the agricultural system), with a new Greek-style fiscal regime lightly overlaid on top.

Today, as in antiquity, the population of Egypt is densely concentrated in a narrow strip of land along the lower Nile valley, with uninhabitable deserts to both east and west. This unforgiving geography makes Egypt, in the words of the economic historian Joseph Manning, 'perhaps the easiest place on earth to tax'. Ptolemaic tax revenue may have attained 15 per cent of GDP, a startlingly high level by pre-modern standards. The long reign of Ptolemy II Philadelphus (283–246 BC) saw a major programme of land reclamation and settlement in the Fayyum (a huge depression west of the Nile, south of Cairo), which was implanted with Greek military settlers (*klērouchoi* or 'plot-holders'), assigned regular plots of land according to their rank. The tax-revenues of the Nile valley and the Fayyum fuelled the explosive growth of the new Ptolemaic capital of Alexandria, the New York of the Hellenistic world. By the first century BC, Alexandria was the biggest city anywhere on earth, with an urban population of perhaps half a million.

Outside Egypt, the Ptolemies ruled over a shifting archipelago of maritime and coastal territories, including (at different times) the Levantine coastal strip, Cyprus, the southern and western coasts of Asia Minor, the Aegean islands, and Cyrenaica (eastern Libya). This maritime empire reached its widest extent in the 270s and 260s BC, when Ptolemy II enjoyed all but undisputed control of the Aegean basin. But—again in stark contrast to the Seleucid realm—the overseas territories were never conceived as an integral part of the Ptolemaic kingdom. Cyprus was governed as a separate principality by a Ptolemaic *stratēgos* ('general'), and the islands of the Aegean were grouped into a federal League of Islanders, headed up by a *nēsiarchos* ('island-commander') appointed by Ptolemy. It is telling that Ptolemaic coinage (struck on a distinctive local weight-standard) seems never to have been used in the Ptolemies' Aegean possessions.

From the 270s to the 160s, the Seleucids and the Ptolemies were locked in a continuous struggle for control of the Levantine coast (the six 'Syrian Wars'). The most dramatic Ptolemaic successes came in 246/5 BC, when the young Ptolemy III Euergetes (reigned 246–222 BC) swept the Seleucids out of Syria, drove eastwards into Mesopotamia, and briefly captured Babylon. One of the most vivid texts from third-century Egypt is an inscription (now lost) from Adulis

31

Seleucid Asia—it was a sign of things to come: between 217 and 186 BC, Egypt would be locked in a near-continuous state of civil war. None of the later Ptolemies (with the partial exception of Cleopatra, in the dying days of the dynasty) came close to reviving the glories of the mid-third century.

The smallest of the three major kingdoms was that of the Antigonids of Macedon. When Antigonus Gonatas (reigned 276–239 BC) came to power in Macedon in 276, he inherited a small rump state, exhausted by years of anarchy and civil war. Between 280 and 278, Macedonia had been devastated by a massive invasion of nomadic Galatian Celts migrating southwards from the Danubian basin. The Galatians penetrated as far south as Delphi before finally being checked in a great battle, fought in a whirling snowstorm, at the very gates of the sanctuary. (The Galatian invaders eventually crossed into Asia and settled on the high Anatolian plateau around Ankara, where they continued to cause trouble for generations to come.) Two years after Antigonus' accession, the tottering Macedonian kingdom was once again overrun, this time by the warlike Pyrrhus, king of the rugged highland kingdom of Epirus (modern Albania and north-west Greece).

From these unpromising beginnings, Antigonus gradually re-established Macedonian control across much of the Greek mainland. Antigonus had inherited a handful of great fortresses in southern Greece (Corinth, Chalcis, Demetrias), and a sustained attempt by Sparta and Athens to drive the Macedonians out of Greece (the 'Chremonidean War', c. 267–262 BC) ended in total victory for Antigonus: the

Athenians spent the next three decades (262–229 BC) under Macedonian occupation. At an uncertain date, perhaps also around 262 BC, Antigonus' fleet destroyed the Ptolemaic navy at the battle of Cos, heralding a new era of Antigonid dominance in the Aegean.

But even at the peak of Antigonid power, much of the Greek mainland remained stubbornly independent. The Aetolian League, initially a small tribal confederation in the mountains west of Delphi, had transformed itself by the mid-third century BC into a formidable anti-Macedonian coalition stretching across central Greece. Further to the south, the Achaean League, a federal alliance of Greek cities in the northern Peloponnese, made a series of spectacular (if short-lived) gains at Antigonus' expense in the 240s and 230s, most famously the daring commando raid on Corinth in 243 BC mentioned in the introduction to Chapter 2. These new federal states (*koina*) in central and southern Greece were one of the great constitutional innovations of the Hellenistic world (and later served as a model for the Founding Fathers of the United States)—an attractive 'third way' between the autonomous Greek city-state and the autocratic Hellenistic kingdom.

West of the Adriatic, in Italy, Sicily, and the western Mediterranean, the influence of Macedon was far less strongly felt. The ancient Greek city-states of Sicily and southern Italy were untouched by the conquests of Philip II and Alexander the Great, and the sole concerted attempt by a Hellenistic monarch to expand his realm to the west, the campaigns of Pyrrhus of Epirus in Italy and Sicily (280–275 BC), ended in complete failure. That said, the third-century kings of

Syracuse in eastern Sicily (Agathocles, 316–289 BC; Hieron II, 269–215 BC) consistently presented themselves as dynastic peers of the Antigonid, Seleucid, and Ptolemaic kings in the eastern Mediterranean, and the court of Hieron at Syracuse was home to a constellation of literary and scientific figures (the poet Theocritus; the mathematician Archimedes) hardly less distinguished than the scholars of the museum at Alexandria. But on the whole, the western Mediterranean took its own path in the third century BC, dominated not by Macedonian kings, but by the imperial city-state of Carthage in modern Tunisia, and, increasingly, by the ambitions of an aggressive new power in central Italy.

Symplokē, 220–188 BC

For the Greek historian Polybius, writing in the mid-second century BC, the 140th Olympiad (220–216 BC) marked a turning point in world history:

> In earlier times, world events had been, so to speak, dispersed, since the various deeds of men showed no unity of initiative, outcomes, or geography. But from this point on, history started to be an organic whole, and the affairs of Italy and Africa became interwoven with those of Asia and of the Greeks, all of them now tending towards a single end.

This 'interweaving' (in Greek, *symplokē*) was the work of Rome. In the course of the third century, the Romans had extended their dominium along the western flank of the Adriatic, and by 219 most of the Greek and Illyrian cities on the eastern shore of the Adriatic (modern Croatia and

Albania) had become an informal Roman protectorate. In 218, the Carthaginian general Hannibal invaded Italy, and the youthful new Antigonid ruler of Macedon, Philip V (221–179 BC), seized his chance to drive Rome out of the eastern Adriatic, and restore Macedonian power across the Balkan peninsula. The First Macedonian War (214–205 BC) saw Philip fighting against a rag-tag anti-Macedonian coalition of Rome, the Aetolian League, and other mainland Greek states; the outcome was an uneasy stalemate, but Rome was now inextricably tied up in mainland Greek affairs. Many Greeks feared for the future: as a Rhodian speaker put it, in an address to the Aetolians recorded by Polybius (207 BC):

> You say that you are fighting against Philip on the Greeks' behalf, so that they might be liberated and not have to follow his orders, but in fact you are fighting for the enslavement and ruin of Greece . . . For once the Romans disentangle themselves from the war with Hannibal in Italy, they will throw themselves with all their force on the lands of Greece, on the pretext of helping the Aetolians against Philip, but with the real intention of subjugating the whole country to themselves.

As we will see, events bore this gloomy prediction out.

In the immediate wake of their victory over Hannibal (201 BC), Rome provoked a second war with Antigonid Macedon (200–197 BC), and the Roman general Flamininus won a crushing victory over Philip V at the battle of Kynoskephalai (197 BC). Antigonid power was broken for good, and Philip's kingdom was confined to his Macedonian homeland. In 196 BC, at the Isthmian Games at Corinth, Flamininus proclaimed the freedom of the Greeks, to general rejoicing. Gold coins minted in Greece at this point depict Flamininus in the style of a charismatic Hellenistic monarch (see Figure 4). Evidently the Greeks did not quite know what to make of their new, powerful western neighbours: Flamininus was an annual elected magistrate, not a Roman king. After 196, the cult of a new deity, the goddess Roma (a personification of Roman power), sprang up in numerous cities of the Greek world. The cult of Roma was apparently modelled on the earlier cults of Hellenistic kings, beautifully illustrating the Greeks' desire to accommodate the new Roman power into their existing world-view.

By the mid-190s, the Romans already had their sights fixed further east. The last decades of the third century had seen a remarkable Seleucid resurgence under Antiochus III

Figure 4 The Roman general Flamininus, depicted in the style of a Hellenistic monarch, with a Nike ('Victory') figure laying a wreath on his name.

(reigned 223–187 BC). In the early years of Antiochus' reign, the Seleucid kingdom must have seemed on the verge of breaking up altogether, with one rebel king (Molon) creating a breakaway state in Babylonia, Persis, and Media, and another (Achaeus) seizing what remained of Seleucid Asia Minor. Over twenty-five years of constant warfare, Antiochus gradually reimposed Seleucid authority from the Aegean to the Hindu Kush. A spectacular series of campaigns in the Far East (212–204 BC) reduced the independent kings of Bactria and Parthia to the status of Seleucid vassals, and between 203 and 196, Antiochus (initially in concert with Philip V) swept the Ptolemies out of the Levant and coastal Asia Minor. By the mid-190s, Antiochus' kingdom was scarcely inferior to the empire of Seleucus I at its peak in 281 BC.

The crash, when it came, was brutal. Between 196 and 192, the Romans, in their new-found capacity as protectors of the freedom of the Greeks, presented Antiochus with an increasingly peremptory series of demands over his treatment of Greek cities under his rule in western Asia Minor. An ill-judged intervention by Antiochus in mainland Greece in 192 sparked a massive and instant Roman retaliation, and in the winter of 190/189 BC, the Roman general Scipio Asiaticus wiped out the Seleucid royal army at the battle of Magnesia in western Turkey (near modern Manisa). Under the terms of the treaty of Apamea (188 BC), Antiochus was ordered to give up all his territory in the Asia Minor peninsula, and to pay Rome a crippling indemnity. In less than a decade, Rome had ruthlessly asserted her dominance over two of the three great powers of the Hellenistic world.

In one of his most haunting poems, *The Battle of Magnesia*, the Alexandrian poet C. P. Cavafy (1863–1933) imagines the news of Antiochus' defeat arriving at the court of the embittered Philip V in Macedon:

He's lost his former ardour, his audacity.
To his tired, almost ailing body,

he'll mainly devote attention. And the remainder
of his life will pass without a care. So Philip

at least maintains. Tonight he plays dice;
he's eager for amusements. On the table

let's put a lot of roses! What of it, if Antiochus
met ruin in Magnesia. They say disaster

fell on the splendid army's multitudes.
They might have exaggerated; it cannot all be true.

Let's hope so; for though an enemy, they were of our race.
Well! One 'let's hope so' is enough. Maybe too much!

Philip, of course, will not postpone the feast.
No matter how intense has been his life's exhaustion,

one good thing he's retained: he hasn't lost his memory at all.
He recalls just how they wept in Syria, what sort of sorrow

they feigned when their mother Macedonia was humbled.–
Let the banquet begin. Slaves: the flutes, the lights.

The 'Short' Second Century, 188–133 BC

Rome's victories over Philip V and Antiochus III redrew the political map of the eastern Mediterranean. In the short term, the chief beneficiaries of the treaty of Apamea (188 BC) were the powerful island city of Rhodes and the Attalid dynasts of Pergamon in north-west Turkey, both of whom had fought on the Roman side in the wars against Philip and Antiochus. The rich Seleucid territories in western Asia Minor were carved up between Rhodes and the Attalids. Rome's decision to grant Rhodes her own miniature 'empire' in south-west Asia Minor (188–167 BC) was particularly startling: it had been centuries since any Greek *polis* had enjoyed this kind of regional hegemony. No Roman officials were yet stationed east of the Adriatic, but it was left quite clear that Rome would no longer tolerate too much independent thinking.

The Attalid kingdom of Pergamon was a small independent principality in the far north-west of the Asia Minor peninsula, not much larger—at least before 188—than a big Greek city-state. But the third-century rulers of Pergamon already aspired to Hellenistic great-power status. Attalus I (reigned 241–197 BC) built up a reputation as an exemplary philhellenic ruler, through lavish and expensive building works at the major cultural centres of the old Greek world (Delphi, Delos, and Athens). In particular, Attalus emphasized the role of the Pergamene kings as protectors of the Greek cities of Asia Minor against the Galatians, the fierce Celtic tribal peoples who had settled in central Turkey in the 270s BC. Several vivid sculptural depictions of defeated Galatians, surviving in Roman copies, are probably modelled on Pergamene originals of the late third or early second century BC (see Figure 5).

In 188 BC, more or less overnight, the able Eumenes II of Pergamon (reigned 197–159 BC) saw his kingdom expanded tenfold at Seleucid expense. In the decades after the treaty of

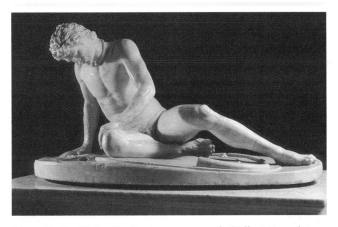

Figure 5 The 'Dying Gaul', a Roman copy of a Hellenistic sculpture depicting a Galatian warrior.

Apamea, Eumenes and his successors built a stable and prosperous state in western Asia Minor. Thanks to the Romans' declared policy of freedom for the Greeks, the old Greek towns of coastal Asia Minor were treated with conspicuous courtesy by the later Attalid kings, and the peninsula's rich agrarian heartlands were seeded with dozens of new city-foundations. Eumenes deliberately sought to present his kingdom as more like the Achaean and Aetolian federations in mainland Greece than the absolutist Ptolemaic and Seleucid monarchies—as, in many ways, it really was. The 'short' Attalid century in Asia Minor (188–133 BC) saw a major boom in public building projects across western and southern Turkey, including perhaps the single best-known monument from the Hellenistic world, the Great Altar of Pergamon,

41

now on display in all its baroque splendour in the Pergamon Museum in Berlin.

The disintegration of the great Hellenistic kingdoms of the East continued. The reigns of Ptolemy IV (221–204 BC) and Ptolemy V (204–180 BC) had seen Egypt rocked by a series of native Egyptian uprisings; upper Egypt was ruled for almost twenty years (206–186 BC) as an independent Pharaonic state. Stripped of most of its overseas possessions by Antiochus III in 203–196 BC, the Ptolemaic kingdom of Egypt must have seemed on the verge of collapse, and in the winter of 170/169 BC the Seleucid Antiochus IV (reigned 175–164 BC) launched a devastating invasion of Egypt. By spring 168, all of lower Egypt except the capital city of Alexandria was under Seleucid control. Once again, the Romans stepped in. A Roman ambassador, Popilius Laenas, met Antiochus IV in the outer suburbs of Alexandria, and presented him with a blunt ultimatum: immediate withdrawal from Egypt, or war with Rome. The memory of the Seleucid defeat at Magnesia two decades earlier was enough to force Antiochus into a humiliating climbdown. The failure of Antiochus' Egyptian expedition marked the beginning of a slow and agonizing decline of Seleucid power in the Near East. A major Jewish revolt under Judas Maccabeus (167–160 BC) ended in the establishment of an independent Hasmonean state in the Levant; more seriously, the old Seleucid heartlands in Mesopotamia were lost to the Parthians between 141 and 138 BC. By the later second century, the Seleucid kingdom was reduced to a small rump state in northern Syria focussed on the city of Antioch.

The year 168 BC also saw the end of the Antigonid kingdom of Macedon. The last Antigonid king, Perseus (reigned 179–168 BC), despite making no open moves against Rome, had rebuilt good relations with the Greek cities of the mainland and Aegean, on a populist platform of debt-cancellation and support of democratic factions against pro-Roman civic elites. The Romans had no intention of allowing Perseus to re-establish Antigonid primacy in mainland Greece, and launched a vicious and unprovoked war against Macedon in 171 BC (the 'Third Macedonian War'). Perseus' army was destroyed at the battle of Pydna in June 168, and the victorious Roman general, Aemilius Paullus, showed no mercy to Greek 'fellow-travellers'. More than a thousand Greek politicians of unsound views were deported to Italy (the historian Polybius among them); 550 leading Aetolians were butchered in their own council-chamber, and 150,000 Epirote Greeks were sold into slavery.

The last major independent power in mainland Greece was the Achaean League, which by now incorporated most of the Greek cities of the Peloponnese under a single federal umbrella. Some modern scholars have been tempted to romanticize the Achaean League, with its unshaking commitment to (in Polybius' words) 'the freedom of the individual cities and the unity of the Peloponnesians'; they may even be right to do so. In 147, the Romans decided to liquidate this last bastion of Greek independence, once again on the flimsiest of pretexts. The Achaean War of 146 BC was brutally short: fifty years after Flamininus had declared the 'freedom of the Greeks' at Corinth, the Roman general Lucius Mummius burned the city to the ground and enslaved its surviving inhabitants.

For most people in the Aegean world, the twin hammer-blows of 168 and 146 marked less of a turning point than one might have expected. Roman dominance in Greece was now unchallenged: some regions (certainly Macedon, perhaps Achaea) were required to pay annual tribute to Rome, and the island of Delos, assigned the status of a free trade port by the Romans in 166 BC, did a brisk trade in slaves for Italy. But Roman jurisdiction east of the Adriatic was still more or less non-existent; the cities of Greece continued to govern their own internal affairs with minimal interference from Rome. The mid-second century BC is often conceived as the age of the 'Roman conquest of Greece'—a strange kind of conquest, which left most of the Greek states autonomous and free from taxation!

In Asia Minor, an era came to an end with the death of the last Attalid king, Attalus III (reigned 138–133 BC). In his will, it was found that he had bequeathed his kingdom to the Roman people. In the fifty-five years between the treaty of Apamea and the bequest of Attalus, the Greek-speaking world had undergone momentous changes. The Antigonid and Attalid kingdoms had ceased to exist; the Seleucid empire was now just one among several squabbling regional principalities in the Near East, and the Ptolemaic dynasty had been reduced to the status of Roman clients. The late second and first centuries BC would see the gradual transformation of this loose network of Roman dependencies and client kingdoms in the eastern Mediterranean into a coherent landscape of directly administered Roman provinces.

The End of the Hellenistic World, 133–30 BC

In the event, it took the Romans four years to bring the Attalid kingdom firmly under their control. A pretender to the Attalid throne, Aristonikos, raised an army of poor Greeks and freed slaves, whom he called *Heliopolitai*, 'Citizens of the Sun'; not until 129 BC was this abortive social revolution finally put down by Roman arms. The rich valleys of western Asia Minor were then re-organized as a new Roman province of Asia, subjected to crippling exploitation by Roman tax-farmers. It was the formation of the province of Asia in the 120s BC, not the dramatic military victories of 168 or 146, which really marked the beginning of direct Roman rule in the Greek world.

Further to the east, the eclipse of the Attalids and the decline in Seleucid authority allowed several local dynasties of northern and eastern Anatolia to emerge as strong regional powers. Huge stretches of central Anatolia were subject to the Ariarathid dynasty of Cappadocia, and Tigranes II of Armenia (ruled *c.* 95–56 BC) carved out an enormous (if short-lived) empire stretching from the Caspian Sea to northern Syria. Most important of all was the kingdom of Pontus, on the Black Sea coast of Turkey, ruled in this period by the fearsome Mithradates VI Eupator (119–63 BC). Over the first three decades of his reign, much of the Black Sea and eastern Anatolia were brought under Pontic control, culminating in the dazzling successes of 88 BC, when Mithradates took the Roman province of Asia by storm.

As coin-portraits of Mithradates indicate (see Figure 6), the king presented himself as a second Alexander the Great, a

Figure 6 King Mithradates VI of Pontus.

charismatic, philhellenic warrior-king in the old Hellenistic mould (Chapter 3). After a generation of vampiric Roman profiteering, the Greeks found this irresistible. Most (though not all) of the Greek cities of Asia welcomed Mithradates as a liberator, and early May 88 BC saw a co-ordinated massacre of all the Romans and Italians in the province, some 80,000 in total. In mainland Greece, Athens too came over to the Mithradatic cause; by the end of the year, most of the Aegean was under Pontic control. The Roman reconquest of the East was entrusted to the general Sulla, who sacked Athens in March 86 BC, and drove Mithradates out of Asia the following year. It is telling that many cities in Roman Asia Minor began to employ a new 'Sullan Era', starting from 85 BC: for many people at the time, Sulla's reorganization of the province was seen as the true beginning of direct Roman rule in Asia.

Sporadic hostilities between Rome and Mithradates dragged on until the mid-60s BC (the king eventually committed suicide, in exile from his kingdom, in 63 BC). But the Romans had learned the lesson of 88 BC: no Hellenistic king would again be allowed to wield as much power as Mithradates. In 65/64 BC, the Roman general Pompey the Great annexed a wide swathe of the East to the Roman empire. New provinces of Bithynia–Pontus and Cilicia were created in eastern Anatolia; the moribund Seleucid kingdom was unceremoniously dissolved and replaced by a new Roman province of Syria. A new constellation of reliably pro-Roman client kings was set in place across the remainder of the Greek East.

By the mid-first century BC, the only surviving independent Hellenistic kingdom of any importance was Ptolemaic Egypt. Long plagued by dynastic strife and internal unrest, the Ptolemaic state inherited by Cleopatra VII in 51 BC had been whittled back to the borders of the old Achaemenid Persian satrapy of Egypt taken over by Ptolemy I in 323 BC. For two decades, Cleopatra waged a campaign of the utmost diplomatic ingenuity to prevent her kingdom falling into Roman hands. Her nine-month love affair with Julius Caesar in 48–47 BC bore immediate fruit in the form of the restoration of Cyprus to the Ptolemaic kingdom, not to mention the birth of a half-Roman son, Ptolemy XV Caesar (known to history as 'Caesarion'). After Caesar's assassination, Cleopatra hitched her kingdom's fortunes to Mark Antony, whose reorganization of Rome's eastern provinces in 37/6 BC saw vast tracts of the Roman East handed over to the Ptolemaic kingdom. Antony clearly intended to rule the eastern Mediterranean as a single, Hellenistic-style Romano-Ptolemaic dominion, presided over by himself and Cleopatra. These grandiose dreams were swept away by Octavian, the future Augustus, through his victory over Antony at the sea-battle of Actium in September 31 BC; Alexandria fell to Octavian eleven months later, and Egypt was smoothly incorporated into the Roman empire.

With Octavian's annexation of Egypt, the whole western half of Alexander's empire up to the Euphrates river was now in Roman hands. The eastern parts of the old Macedonian empire were controlled by the Parthians, the Iranian dynasty who had succeeded the Seleucids in Mesopotamia and Iran in the course of the second century BC. The Greek city-states, and Greek culture more widely, continued to survive and flourish under Roman (and Parthian) rule. Several of the minor client-dynasties of the Near East, the direct successors to the great Hellenistic kingdoms, persisted into the Julio–Claudian period and beyond. But if one had to name a time and place at which the curtain fell on the Hellenistic world, then most people would surely opt for Alexandria on 12 August, 30 BC. As Cleopatra's servant Iras puts it in Shakespeare's *Antony and Cleopatra*, 'The bright day is done,/ And we are for the dark'.

Demetrius the Besieger and Hellenistic Kingship

Warlords and Kings

In the early summer of 307 BC, a young Macedonian general set sail from Ephesus with a fleet of 250 warships. Demetrius, some thirty years of age, and later affectionately known as 'the Besieger', was not of royal blood. His father Antigonus the One-Eyed had been a minor member of the Macedonian royal court, rising to power only after Alexander's death, thanks to his command of the main bulk of the Macedonian army in Asia. By 307, Antigonus had seized control of most of Alexander's conquered territories in western Asia, and now had his single eye fixed on the wealthy cities of mainland Greece. Demetrius' mission in 307 was the 'liberation' of the cities of Greece from the Macedonian dynast Cassander, Antigonus' chief rival for control of the Aegean.

Demetrius sailed first against the city of Athens, ruled since 317 by Cassander's client Demetrius of Phalerum, a conservative philosopher from Aristotle's Peripatetic school. In June 307, the Besieger's fleet sailed unchallenged into the Piraeus, the main harbour of Athens. His arrival was unexpected. Plutarch, in his *Life of Demetrius*, tells us that the Athenians had mistaken his armada for that of Cassander's ally Ptolemy of Egypt; the Aegean was bristling with Macedonian warships in those days. The deposed Demetrius of Phalerum came to terms with the city's new master, leaving Athens on the following day for Thebes. He eventually ended his days, like many Greek intellectuals of the period, in Ptolemy's court at Alexandria.

The new regime at Athens started with a bang. For ten years, Athens had been governed by Cassander as a narrow oligarchy. Demetrius now restored the ancestral Athenian democracy (at least in name), and promised the Athenians vast gifts of grain and ship-timber from his father's domains in Asia. The Athenians promptly hailed Demetrius as their saviour and benefactor; Demetrius and Antigonus were given the titles of Saviour Gods, and on the spot where Demetrius had first alighted from his chariot on arriving in Athens, the Athenians consecrated an altar to Demetrius the Alighter. Most important of all, as Plutarch tells us, 'the Athenians were the first among all men to address Demetrius and Antigonus as Kings, although both had previously shrunk from using the title'.

The first, but not the last. A year later, after a stunning victory by Demetrius over Ptolemy's fleet off Cyprus, both Demetrius and Antigonus were formally acclaimed as kings by their army. Within three years of Demetrius' capture of Athens, another five men had claimed the title of 'king' for themselves: Seleucus in Babylon, Ptolemy in Egypt, Lysima-chus in Thrace, Cassander in Macedon, and Agathocles in Sicily. As the Hellenistic period wore on, monarchs continued to multiply, particularly in the lands vacated by the steadily shrinking Seleucid kingdom in Asia; by the early second century BC, the Asia Minor peninsula alone was home to a good half a dozen local dynasts bearing the royal title.

What claim did men like Demetrius and Antigonus have to the title of king? In purely legal or constitutional terms, none whatsoever. Demetrius had no connection to the old Macedonian royal line; he and his father were essentially warlords, regional strongmen who could command an army's loyalty. But the Athenians were not wrong to recognize Demetrius as a king. A medieval Greek lexicon, the so-called *Suda*, states the matter most pithily in its short entry on kingship (*'basileia'*):

> Monarchical powers are given to men neither by nature nor by law; they are given to those who are capable of commanding troops and handling politics competently. Such was the case with the successors to Alexander.

Kingship in the early Hellenistic world was primarily a matter of power. Demetrius was a man of outstanding charisma, dazzling military success, and colossal personal wealth, and therefore—in the eyes of his subjects, which is all that matters—he deserved the title of king. An impoverished, peace-loving or unsuccessful king was a contradiction in terms: early Hellenistic kings were expected to look and behave like the young Demetrius, handsome and radiant, rich and warlike, fighting on horseback at the head of his troops. The new generation of kings drew heavily, of course, on the glamorous and dynamic generalship of Alexander the Great; but Alexander's royal authority had always rested first and foremost on his hereditary position as 'national' monarch of the Macedonians. Not so Demetrius.

As we might expect, the institutional position of these new-style Hellenistic monarchs was rather poorly defined. Their courts were made up of informal circles of friends (*'philoi'*), and the fiscal and administrative structures of the new kingdoms were rudimentary to say the least. Monarchy in the late fourth and early third century was personal, not territorial. None of the successor monarchs ever described themselves as kings 'of' a particular region: they were simply 'kings'. Significantly, when Demetrius lost almost all of his dependent territories after the battle of Ipsus in 301 BC, and his 'kingdom' was reduced to a few maritime fortresses (Ephesus, Corinth, Tyre), he did not cease to be a king: so long as he retained his formidable war-fleet, his royal status was not in question.

As one generation succeeded another in the newly established Hellenistic kingdoms, the charismatic warlords of the late fourth century were gradually replaced by hereditary monarchs. Personal kingship was steadily transformed into a more stable territorial and dynastic kingship. But the origins of the Hellenistic monarchies in warfare, wealth, and personal magnetism were never forgotten. Right down to the end of the Hellenistic period, kings were always depicted in much the same way, as glamorous and dynamic heroes, taking on Alexander's mantle as warriors and conquerors.

The so-called 'Terme ruler', an above-life-size bronze statue of a second-century Hellenistic ruler (now in the Palazzo Massimo alle Terme in Rome), shows the king as a muscle-bound superman, powerful and ruthless, ready for new conquests (see Figure 7).

The King at War

War was at the heart of Hellenistic kingship. The acclamation of Demetrius and Antigonus as kings by their army followed hard on the heels of Demetrius' great naval victory over Ptolemy off Cyprus (306 BC), and almost a century later, some time in the 230s BC, the local dynast Attalus of Pergamon used a major victory over the Galatians of central Asia Minor as his justification for claiming the title of king. Numerous Hellenistic kings carried royal epithets or nicknames like *Nikēphoros*, 'victory-bearer', *Kallinikos*, 'winner of fair victories', or *Anikētos*, 'invincible'. A good Hellenistic king was expected to defend his inheritance, expand his territory by conquest, and enrich his army with a regular supply of booty.

The relentless militarism of Hellenistic monarchy has its origins in the carnage out of which the new kingdoms emerged. For thirty years after Alexander's death, vast armies, liberally funded by the booty captured from the Persian royal treasuries by Alexander, fought their way back and forth across Asia and Europe. Between 320 and 309 BC, Antigonus the One-Eyed (not a man in the first flush of youth) was on campaign almost without pause: against Eumenes in Asia Minor, Mesopotamia, and Iran

Figure 7 The 'Terme ruler', a bronze statue of an unidentified Hellenistic prince, from the Quirinal in Rome; the statue was probably taken to Rome as booty some time in the second or first century BC.

(320–316), against a coalition of Ptolemy, Cassander, and Lysimachus in the Levant and Asia Minor (315–311), and finally against Seleucus in Mesopotamia (310–309). Antigonus himself died on the battlefield in 301 BC, still fighting in person well into his eighty-second year. In this grim struggle for land and prestige, the successor dynasts ploughed all their resources into the arts of war: the first Seleucid king, Seleucus I Nicator ('the Conqueror'), was willing to give up his territorial possessions in India to Chandragupta Maurya in return for 500 war elephants.

The most dramatic of all the campaigns waged by the early Hellenistic kings was Demetrius' great siege of the island-city of Rhodes, conducted over an entire year from summer 305 to summer 304 BC. Rhodes, probably the most powerful city-state in the Greek world at this period, had remained formally neutral in the wars of the successors, but showed particular favour to Ptolemy, since much of Rhodes' wealth (and all of her grain-supply) came through maritime trade with Egypt. When the Rhodians showed insufficient willingness to support Antigonus in his war against Ptolemy, Demetrius sailed against the city with a vast armament of more than 370 ships, 40,000 infantry, and an unspecified number of cavalry and pirate allies. Demetrius launched repeated assaults against the Rhodians' walls by land and sea, employing an increasingly Heath Robinson-esque array of siege engines (hence his nickname 'the Besieger'). The most elaborate of these was his famous *helepolis* ('City-Taker'), an armoured siege-tower nine stories high, and so heavy that it required 3,400 men to push it forwards on its 3-foot-thick iron-plated wheels.

For all its strategic importance, Rhodes was certainly not worth the colossal expenditure of resources that Demetrius sank into the siege. The capture of the city rapidly became a matter of personal prestige for Demetrius, not least because the besieged Rhodians continued to be supplied with grain by his three main rivals, Cassander, Lysimachus, and above all Ptolemy, who also sent mercenary forces in support of the city. Demetrius' increasingly extravagant gadgets had something of the theatrical about them: they were a means of impressing the wider Greek world with his unlimited resources of money, human capital, and military power. All to no avail—the city did not fall, and Demetrius, exhausted, finally broke off the siege after a year's effort. The Rhodians sold off the siege equipment left behind, and used the proceeds to build the famous Colossus of Rhodes, one of the Seven Wonders of the World, a titanic bronze statue (30 metres tall) of the sun-god Helios. The Colossus stood for fifty-four years overlooking the harbour of Rhodes, a warning to any Hellenistic king tempted to emulate Demetrius' disastrous military over-ambition.

Demetrius the God

The cities of the Greek world had never had to deal with anything quite like Demetrius before. Some Greeks, such as the Ionians of western Asia Minor, had lived for long periods under the rule of the Persian Achaemenid kings, distant barbarian rulers who intervened very little in the affairs of their subject cities (aside from taxing them). But Demetrius and his rivals were kings of a very different kind. They were

Greek, or at least Macedonian; they possessed massive coercive power, and were prepared to use it to the benefit or disfavour of Greek cities. What is more, they could be highly visible presences in the life of Greek communities: Demetrius himself resided at Athens for several months at a time in the winters of 304/3 and 303/2, living in outrageously dissolute fashion in the rear chamber of the Parthenon itself (much to the Athenians' disgust). The Greeks needed to find a new way of structuring their relationship with these potent and charismatic supermen. The way that they chose was to worship them as gods.

This is less surprising than it might seem at first sight. The Greeks—unlike, say, Christians or Muslims—had never placed a high premium on individual religious conviction ('belief'). Greek religion was an eminently social phenomenon, based on collective rituals—festivals, sacrifices, processions—performed by the entire community. Theology had never interested Greeks very much, and 'faith' was not a salient category in Greek thought. The crucial thing was the reciprocal relationship between men and gods, mediated through prayer and animal sacrifice: we offer you cattle, and you protect us from plague and disaster.

The Hellenistic kings—men of godlike power and status— were prepared to offer reciprocal benefits of precisely this kind. If a city was struck down by an earthquake, or threatened by a foreign army, Demetrius really could rebuild your temples or protect your walls in return for your collective loyalty and dependence. The precise metaphysical character of the kings was simply not that important: worshipping Demetrius as a god did not necessarily involve holding any alarming beliefs about his bodily fabric, projected life-span, or ability to wield thunderbolts. If Demetrius responded favourably to the correct performance of rituals, then he *really was*, in all important respects, a god just like Zeus or Apollo.

In 291 or 290 BC, Demetrius arrived at Athens during the celebration of a major religious festival, the Eleusinian Mysteries of Demeter and Kore (Persephone). The Athenians greeted the king with an elaborate religious ceremony, burning incense to him on altars and offering libations. A Dionysiac chorus of men wearing erect phalluses came to meet Demetrius in the streets of Athens; the hymn that they sung to him survives, and reads as follows:

How the greatest and dearest of the gods are present in our city! For a single moment has brought Demeter and Demetrius together here: she comes to celebrate the solemn mysteries of Kore [the Eleusinian Mysteries], while he is here in joy, as is fitting for the god, fair and laughing. His appearance is numinous; his friends are all around him, and he in their midst, as though his friends were stars and he the sun. Hail, child of the most powerful god Poseidon and of Aphrodite! For other gods are either far away, or do not have ears, or do not exist, or take no notice of us, but you we see present here, not made of wood or stone, but real. So we pray to you: first make peace, dearest; for you have the power. That Sphinx who holds sway not over Thebes but over the whole of Greece, the Aetolian, who sits on a rock like the ancient Sphinx, who seizes and carries away all our people, against whom I cannot fight (for it is an Aetolian custom to seize their neighbours' property, and now even that of far-off peoples)—best of all, punish her yourself; if not, find some

Oedipus who will either hurl that Sphinx down from the rocks or reduce her to ashes.

The prayer with which the hymn concludes is a strikingly practical one. The Aetolians of central Greece have been raiding Athenian territory; the Athenians pray to Demetrius to launch a retaliatory campaign against them, either in person or by sending one of his generals ('some Oedipus'). The Athenians clearly saw no incongruity in invoking Demetrius as a god, 'not made of wood or stone, but real', and simultaneously asking for military help against the Aetolians. What seems to us like a standard piece of international diplomacy—an appeal to a stronger power for protection—was expressed by the Athenians as a prayer to a living god.

Kings were not always present in person. Greek cities performed regular sacrificial rituals in honour of absent Hellenistic monarchs, modelled on pre-existing civic cults of the Olympian gods. One of our earliest descriptions of a civic ruler-cult comes from the small city of Aegae, on the west coast of Turkey, where the Seleucid victory over Lysimachus in 281 BC was marked with the establishment of a new temple dedicated to King Seleucus I and his son Antiochus:

So that the Revealed Gods Seleucus and Antiochus should be honoured by men in a manner worthy of their good deeds, let a temple, as beautiful as possible, be built beside the sanctuary of Apollo, with its own surrounding sanctuary. Let two cult statues be dedicated, as beautiful as possible, with the inscriptions 'Seleucus' and 'Antiochus', and let a statue and altar of the Saviour Goddess be erected in front of the temple. Opposite the temple, let an altar be founded, with the words 'Of Seleucus and Antiochus' inscribed on it, and let a sacred precinct, as beautiful as possible, be marked out. During the main annual sacrifice, let bulls be brought into the sanctuary for the Saviours Seleucus and Antiochus, and sacrificed just as for Apollo; and let two sacrifices be performed every month on the day that the city was liberated (by Seleucus and Antiochus). Let the civic tribes be reorganised, so that there should be six instead of four, and let the two new tribes be named 'Seleucis' and 'Antiochis'... And let the hall of the prytanes and the hall of the generals be rebuilt, with that of the prytanes renamed the 'Seleuceion' and that of the generals renamed the 'Antiocheion'.

The new cult of the Seleucid kings is clearly modelled on the existing cult of Apollo at Aegae. Crucially, ruler-worship has not been imposed by the Seleucids: the people of Aegae have introduced the cult of their own accord, as a way of cementing their future relations with their new Seleucid rulers. It is especially interesting to see the city reorganizing its political structure (the civic 'tribes') and even renaming certain public buildings in honour of the Seleucid kings. Likewise, after Demetrius' first capture of Athens in 307 BC, the Athenians created two new tribes named after their royal benefactors, 'Antigonis' and 'Demetrias'. Like the cults of Hellenistic kings, these honorific gestures were symbolic ways of expressing the cities' gratitude and loyalty to their new masters. The cities could of course expect to receive juicy privileges in return—internal autonomy, military protection, exemption from royal taxes, and so forth.

Kings and Cities

In 303 BC, Demetrius' troops captured the small Greek city of Sicyon in the northern Peloponnese. Sicyon was a town with a long history, and had enjoyed some modest international fame in the age of its tyrant dynasty, the Orthagorids, in the early sixth century BC. Late fourth-century Sicyon was a small farming and manufacturing town, lying on a gently sloping coastal plain between the Helisson and Asopus rivers, at the foot of a formidable slice of table-land, protected on all sides by precipitous cliffs. This high plateau caught the Besieger's attention, as being completely impregnable for siege-engines. Demetrius promptly instructed the demolition of the existing town in the plain, and ordered the Sicyonians to relocate their homes to the easily defensible upper acropolis. As the historian Diodorus Siculus relates:

> Demetrius gave help to the mass of citizens in the construction work, and restored their freedom to them, for which benefaction they granted him honours equal to those of the gods. They renamed the city Demetrias, and voted both to celebrate annual sacrifices, festivals, and contests in his honour, and to grant him the other honours due to a city-founder.

The people of Sicyon were not the only Greeks to be forcibly relocated by Demetrius. In northern Greece, near the modern city of Volos, no fewer than fourteen small Greek towns were depopulated to provide the raw manpower for a new royal capital, also named Demetrias. Quite how cavalier Demetrius and his father Antigonus were in their treatment of existing communities can be seen in a long inscription from the Ionian city of Teos, in which Antigonus orders the immediate transfer of the entire population of nearby Lebedos into Teos, in the face of increasingly desperate practical objections from both cities.

In the late fourth and third centuries BC, hundreds of new Graeco-Macedonian cities were founded by the Hellenistic kings across western Eurasia, many of them laid out on a scale hitherto undreamed of in the Greek world. As we saw in Chapter 2, Seleucus I founded four huge new cities in north-west Syria alone (Antioch by Daphne, Apamea on the Orontes, Laodicea by the Sea, Seleucia in Pieria), the first two of which had populations numbering in the hundreds of thousands by the later Hellenistic period. The physical remains of these cities give an unnerving sense of the power and ambition of the early Hellenistic monarchs. In western Asia Minor, the city of Ephesus, refounded by Lysimachus and (temporarily) renamed Arsinoeia after his wife Arsinoe, was planned on a truly spectacular scale: its fortifications, 9 kilometres long, are estimated to have required some 200,000 cubic metres of cut stone for the curtain wall alone.

These new cities served several purposes. Most of them bore the name of their royal founder or members of his family, advertising the dynasty's power and prestige: Egyptian Alexandria and Kandahar in Afghanistan both preserve the name of their founder, Alexander the Great, while Thessaloniki, the second city of modern Greece, was named by the successor monarch Cassander after his wife Thessalonice

(Alexander's half-sister). Many cities were home to large military garrisons: the main highway across Asia Minor was studded with new Seleucid fortress-towns at 40-kilometre intervals, and Demetrias, in northern Greece, became known as one of the 'fetters of Hellas'. In the vast open spaces of Seleucid Asia, the new cities served as centres of bureaucracy and taxation for the budding regime; more than 30,000 administrative seal-impressions have been excavated at Seleucia on the Tigris, the capital of Seleucid Mesopotamia.

On the most practical level of all, the cities served to house a deluge of hopeful migrants from Greece and Macedon into the newly conquered lands of the colonial Near East. Every year, tens of thousands of men and women set out from the old Greek lands for a better life in the 'New World' of Ptolemaic Egypt and Seleucid Asia, swelling the population of mega-cities like Seleucia on the Tigris or Alexandria in Egypt. The kings' personal reputation for generosity, machismo, and loose living was not the least of the enticements drawing people across the sea. In his fourteenth *Idyll*, the poet Theocritus imagines two young Greeks, Aeschines and Thyonichus, planning their getaway to the land of the Ptolemies:

> If you really mean to emigrate, then Ptolemy's the best pay-master for a free man. What sort of fellow is he otherwise? The best there is—considerate, cultured, partial to the ladies, as pleasant as can be, knows who his friends are (and his enemies even better), bestower of great favours upon many, and doesn't refuse when asked, just as a king ought to behave...So, if you fancy clasping the military cloak on

> your right shoulder, and have the guts to stand firm on both
> your feet to meet a strong man's charge, then off with you to
> Egypt.

Theocritus should know: himself a native of Syracuse in
Sicily, he emigrated to Alexandria around 270 BC.

The Royal 'Club'

One of the most striking features of the new royal regimes
was their similarity to one another. Royal coins and portrait
sculpture depict Hellenistic kings and queens in much the
same way, whether they happened to rule in Afghanistan,
Cappadocia, or Sicily. Kings were almost invariably shown
as clean-shaven, with thick wavy hair and a plain diadem
(a kind of narrow headband) marking their royal status (see
Figure 8); all of these elements were taken over from the
official iconography of Alexander the Great. Courts and royal
administration took similar forms pretty much everywhere:

Figure 8 Silver tetradrachm of Demetrius the Besieger.

Attalid financial officials in western Asia Minor carried the same titles as those in the Seleucid kingdom to the East (the *hemiolios*, *epi tōn hierōn*, *dioikētēs*, *eklogistēs*, etc.). Royal letters and edicts were composed in a single, 'international' chancery style, and in cases where the opening lines of a royal letter happen not to have survived (as frequently happens with stone inscriptions), it is often impossible to tell which king was the author.

A king's conduct towards his subjects was governed by certain conventional expectations. Kings were expected to be munificent towards their dependants, to respond to private and public petitions, and to recognize symbolic honours with a generous package of material benefactions (the reciprocal relationship that the Greeks called *euergesia*, the conferral of social status in return for good deeds, discussed further in Chapter 6). A particularly telling anecdote is recounted by Plutarch in his *Life of Demetrius*:

> An old woman once started pestering Demetrius as he was passing by, and repeatedly demanded a hearing. When he replied that he had no time, she screeched back at him 'Then don't be king!' Demetrius was deeply stung, and after reflection returned to his house. He put off all other business, and for many days devoted his time to receiving those who required an audience, beginning with this old woman.

Ben trovato, but unlikely to be true. Precisely the same story is told of King Philip II of Macedon, of Alexander's Macedonian regent Antipater, and of the Roman emperor Hadrian; a somewhat similar story attached itself to Demetrius' older contemporary Seleucus. Clearly we are dealing with a piece of ancient folk wisdom about how a good king *ought* to behave. All Hellenistic monarchs were subject to the same social rules, many of which were inherited by the Roman emperors who eventually succeeded them in the eastern Mediterranean.

This convergence of royal styles and ideology is, at first sight, somewhat surprising. After all, the local circumstances of the Hellenistic kingdoms were very far from uniform (Chapter 2). In Egypt, the Ptolemaic king was pharaoh to several million native Egyptians, who had very different expectations of their rulers; the brother-sister marriage practised by the Ptolemaic dynasty (unthinkable in a traditional Greek or Macedonian context) is only the most obvious concession to traditional pharaonic styles of rule. The third- and second-century Antigonid kings, by contrast, ruled over a fairly uniform 'old world' kingdom of Macedonians and Greeks. The Seleucid kingdom was culturally the most complex of all, being made up of a baffling variety of different Near Eastern peoples (Iranians, Babylonians, Jews, Arabs...), with a relatively small Graeco-Macedonian settler class concentrated in the new Seleucid cities.

But the kingdoms also had a great deal in common. All the kings competed for the services of a vast, itinerant population of mercenary soldiers, many of Greek or Macedonian origin, but also including ever larger numbers of Celts, Thracians, Illyrians, Arabs, and others. Since Hellenistic royal gold and silver coinages were mainly struck in order to pay the wages of these soldiers of fortune, it is hardly surprising that royal coins end up sharing a common 'visual language' of kingship. What is more, although the heartlands of the major kingdoms were culturally very diverse, military rivalry between the dynasties was largely played out in a fairly small and homogeneous region, the Aegean basin and (to a lesser extent) the Levantine coast. To take an extreme instance, between 310 and 280 BC, the coastal cities of Caria in south-west Asia Minor passed from Antigonus to Ptolemy I (309), were regained by Antigonus (308), fell to Lysimachus (301), were briefly reconquered by Demetrius (287), were recovered by Lysimachus (286–285), were lost to Seleucus (281), and at last fell into the hands of Ptolemy II (280–278). Should we be surprised that the kings ended up speaking more or less the same diplomatic language—and offering a fairly similar 'package' of fiscal benefits—to the Greek cities of the region?

Finally, although every now and then a monarch professed a claim to universal rule, in practice the Hellenistic kings saw themselves as peers. Right from the outset, the successor monarchs recognized, implicitly or explicitly, their rivals' claims to royal status. The early Hellenistic dynasts addressed one another as 'king' in their correspondence, and Demetrius' refusal to do so is cited by Plutarch as an instance of his exceptional arrogance and pride:

> Alexander himself never refused the title of King to any other monarch, nor did he call himself King of Kings, even though he himself had granted the title and status of king to many others. But Demetrius used to mock and laugh at those who gave the name of King to anyone but his father and himself, and was delighted to hear people drinking toasts at banquets to King Demetrius, Seleucus the Elephant-Master, Admiral Ptolemy, Lysimachus the Treasurer, and Agathocles the

> Island-Master of Sicily. The other kings, when this was
> reported to them, found his attitude highly amusing.

In fact, even Demetrius was in the end compelled to recognize his position as one monarch among many. In 298, Demetrius was a fleet-commander without a kingdom, and Seleucus was a king without a navy; a formal alliance between the two men was sealed at the coastal town of Rhosus in Turkey (near modern Antakya) by the marriage of Seleucus to Demetrius' daughter Stratonice. The exchanges between the two men, says Plutarch, 'were at once put on a royal footing': Seleucus entertained Demetrius in his army-camp in lavish fashion, before Demetrius received Seleucus on board his vast flagship. By this point, King Lysimachus had already married Ptolemy's daughter Arsinoe, and several marital exchanges between the Seleucid and Ptolemaic dynasties took place in the third and second centuries BC. Each king wielded absolute power in his own domain, but, as in early modern Europe, each monarch was also part of a wider 'royal club', a rich source of potential allies, rivals, and marital partners. After the loss of all his royal territories in mainland Greece (288–287 BC), and a last desperate adventure in Asia Minor (287–285), Demetrius eventually threw himself on Seleucus' mercy, and ended his days in captivity at his son-in-law's court, where he quietly drank himself to death, in the fifty-fifth year of his life.

Eratosthenes and the System of the World

The Chicken-Coop of the Muses

Few aspects of the Hellenistic world have captivated the modern imagination so much as the Museum and Library of Ptolemaic Alexandria. The vision of a dedicated institution of learning and research, populated by librarians, poets, and scholars, and munificently endowed by an enlightened Ptolemaic state, has—for obvious reasons—an irresistible appeal to many modern academics. The first (and only) detailed description of the Museum of Alexandria comes from the geographer Strabo, writing in the early first century AD:

> The Museum is a part of the palace complex, and has a covered walkway, a hall with seats, and a large house containing a common dining-room for the learned men who belong to the Museum. This guild of men have their possessions in common, and there is a priest in charge of the

> Museum, formerly appointed by the king, but today selected
> by Caesar.

As Strabo indicates, the 'Museum' of Alexandria was not, like
modern museums, a collection of physical artefacts, but a
shrine dedicated to the Muses. The scholars attached to the
Museum were housed and fed at state expense, and wrote on
a dazzling variety of subjects, from pure mathematics to the
textual criticism of Homer. The general pedantic ghastliness
of the scholars' guild was already notorious in the Hellenistic era, as indicated by a fragment of the third-century satir-
ist and sceptic Timon of Phlius:

> Plenty of men get free dinners in populous Egypt, those book-
> ish scribblers, arguing away interminably in the chicken-coop
> of the Muses.

It is sobering to reflect on how little hard evidence we have
for the great Alexandrian Library associated with the
Museum. Its precise location is unknown: most historians
assume (or rather guess) that it formed part of the Museum-
complex, no physical remains of which survive. We do not
know when or by whom it was established, although such
evidence as we have seems to point to the early years of the
reign of Ptolemy II Philadelphus (283–246 BC). The figures
given by ancient and medieval authors for the total number
of volumes in the Library (between 200,000 and 700,000)
are demonstrably fantastic: we should be thinking, at most,
of tens of thousands of papyrus rolls, and perhaps consider-
ably fewer. Finally, there is no good reason to think that the
Library was ever destroyed by fire: like most of the libraries of
antiquity, the Alexandrian collection of papyri probably

suffered a slow and unromantic death by human neglect, natural decay, and the work of the common mouse.

Nonetheless, Hellenistic Alexandria was evidently a remarkable centre of intellectual activity. The third and second centuries BC saw spectacular developments in the fields of mathematics, geography, the natural sciences, humanistic scholarship and—not least—poetry, much of which can be attributed to 'bookish scribblers' attached to the Museum at Alexandria. One of the few things that we do know about the Alexandrian Library is that it had a dedicated librarian-in-charge. A papyrus from Oxyrhynchus preserves a list of most of the Hellenistic librarians, and they are all, without exception, intellectuals of the first rank: the poet Apollonius of Rhodes, author of the epic *Argonautica*; Eratosthenes of Cyrene, the greatest polymath of the Hellenistic Age; Aristophanes of Byzantium, the first lexicographer and critical editor of early Greek epic and lyric poetry. In the 'chicken-coop of the Muses', the scholars of Ptolemaic Alexandria quietly transformed man's understanding of his place in the world.

Space and Time: Eratosthenes of Cyrene

Perhaps the single most impressive figure associated with the Museum was the mathematician, astronomer, chronographer, literary critic and poet Eratosthenes of Cyrene (*c.* 276–194 BC). His intellectual interests were so broad that he coined a new term to describe his profession: *philologos*, 'lover of learning'. In antiquity, he was nicknamed 'Beta' (the second letter of the Greek alphabet), since despite his brilliance across a huge range of disciplines, he was only second-best in each of them. There are worse ways to be remembered.

In one field, at least, the title 'Beta' was grossly unjust. The discipline of scientific geography was the single-handed creation of Eratosthenes, whose two major works in the field, *On the Measurement of the Earth* and *Geographika*, brought about a revolution in the Greeks' conception of space and place. In the first of these books, Eratosthenes devised a beautiful method for estimating the circumference of the earth (see Figure 9). Eratosthenes began with three broadly correct assumptions: that the earth is spherical; that

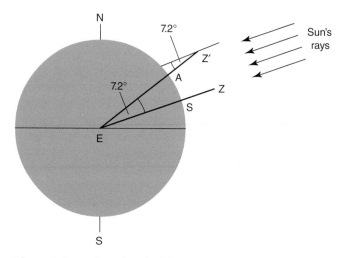

Figure 9 Eratosthenes' method for measuring the circumference of the earth.

continuous geometric space, divided up by latitude and longitude. The inhabited temperate zone, from India to Spain, extended across only a third of the circumference of the earth. (Eratosthenes did not of course guess at the existence of the Americas.) Within this zone, Eratosthenes argued, the traditional Greek division of the world into three continents (Asia, Europe, and Africa, separated by narrow straits like the Hellespont) was an arbitrary human construct. The distinction between Europe and Asia resulted from the fact that the earliest Greeks 'did not have a clear perspective on the whole inhabited world, but only on their own land [mainland Greece] and the Carian land lying opposite, in which the Ionians and their neighbours now live [mainland Turkey]'. Because the Aegean Sea happens to form a clear boundary between Greece and Asia Minor, the Greeks, so Eratosthenes argues, wrongly assumed that there were real *continuous* boundaries between Europe and Asia. In fact, this was false: the inhabited world formed a single whole, and the categories of European 'Greeks' and Asiatic 'barbarians' had no objective geographic basis.

Not the least of Eratosthenes' achievements in the *Geographika* was his cool-headed understanding of what counted as evidence. The first book of the *Geographika* contained an extended discussion of the geographical 'information' preserved in the Homeric epics, the occasion of much learned debate by scholars ancient and modern. For Eratosthenes, Homeric geography was wholly imaginary: any attempt to map, say, Odysseus' journey home from Troy onto the real geography of the Mediterranean was doomed to end in frustration and muddle: 'You will find the scene of

Odysseus' wanderings,' he sarcastically concluded, 'when you track down the cobbler who sewed up the sack of the winds.'

The same sharp critical instincts were on display in Eratosthenes' work on historical chronology. As a glance at almost any page of Herodotus will show, earlier Greek writers had used a very haphazard system for dating historical events, by human generations, the annual civic magistrates of Athens, synchronies with other famous rulers or battles—pretty much whatever fell to hand. Eratosthenes brought order to this chaos. In his *Chronographiai*, he drew up a complete chronological table of Greek history based on the best documentary sources available to him. Surviving lists of winners at the Olympic Games took him back to 776/5 BC, and early Spartan king-lists carried him another three centuries further, to the year 1104/3 BC. He divided up the whole history of the Greek world from the Trojan War (dated by him to 1184/3 BC) to the death of Alexander the Great (323 BC) into ten historical epochs, marked off from one another by significant events (Xerxes' invasion of Greece, the outbreak of the Peloponnesian War, and so forth). Eratosthenes' chronological 'spine' for Greek history, based on Olympiad dating, was adopted by virtually all later Greek historical writers; in certain respects we still depend on it today.

Scientific research does not take place in a vacuum, and Eratosthenes' geographic and historical scholarship was intimately tied up with the interests of his Ptolemaic patrons. It is, at the very least, a striking coincidence that his measurement of the earth was anchored to the northern and southern limits of the Ptolemies' Egyptian domain (Alexandria, the capital city, and Syene, the southern border of Ptolemaic Egypt). Alone among the major Hellenistic dynasties, the third-century Ptolemaic kings ruled over territories in Europe, Asia, and Africa; the shape of the far-flung, cross-continental Ptolemaic empire surely influenced Eratosthenes' denial of any objective divisions between the three continents. Even the Ptolemaic tax system, based on a comprehensive geometric survey of all taxable Egyptian land-holdings, finds distant echoes in Eratosthenes' geometric mapping of the entire inhabited world. None of this is to detract from Eratosthenes' achievement; it ought merely to remind us of his status as a royal appointee, housed and fed in the palace of the Ptolemies at the king's expense.

Pure and Applied: Archimedes of Syracuse

Given the choice, Eratosthenes would probably have wished to have been remembered first and foremost for his work in pure mathematics. Few of Eratosthenes' mathematical writings have survived, aside from a short treatise addressed to Ptolemy IV Philopator on the duplication of the cube (to be discussed presently) and a brief summary of his so-called 'sieve', an elegant algorithm for finding all prime numbers up to a given limit. In truth, 'Beta' seems about right for Eratosthenes' status as a mathematician. There has only ever been one candidate for 'Alpha': Eratosthenes' older contemporary Archimedes of Syracuse (*c.* 287–212 BC), the greatest mathematician of classical antiquity.

Little is known of Archimedes' career. He passed most of his life at Syracuse, the hub of Hellenistic culture in the western Mediterranean, then under the rule of King Hieron II (*c.* 269–215 BC). He and Eratosthenes were friends, or at least long-distance mutual admirers: two of Archimedes' most important surviving works, the *Cattle Problem* and the *Method*, are addressed to Eratosthenes. Archimedes' reputation rests primarily on his status as the founder of mathematical physics, or the application of pure mathematics to real-world physical problems. His treatise *On Floating Bodies*, the first major work in the field of hydrostatics, is concerned with the equilibrium positions of solids of various shapes and densities when floating in water; there is some reason to think that Archimedes had the design of warships' hulls in mind (the Hellenistic period was an age of rapid innovation, and overconfident gigantism, in shipbuilding).

Even when apparently engaged in problems of pure geometry, Archimedes was repeatedly drawn back to the mathematics of the physical world. In his *Method*, he proposed a quite startling means of determining the volume of a geometric object, say a cone or a segment of a sphere. Archimedes asks us, first, to imagine this object as a uniform solid which has been sliced up into a large number—a very large number indeed—of very thin parallel slices perpendicular to its axis. He then invites us to picture these slices as superimposed and suspended at one end of an imaginary lever, in equilibrium with some other solid whose volume and centre of gravity are known, say a cylinder. The eponymous 'Method' is this beautiful application of mechanical methods to geometric problems: placing a complex geometric object in equilibrium with a simpler one on an imaginary balance, and thereby avoiding the difficult integration which would be required to calculate the original object's volume directly. (This approach also involved the earliest attested use of infinitesimals in mathematical argument—a crucial first step towards the discovery of the calculus.)

The Archimedean 'physical turn' in mathematics was entirely in line with wider intellectual trends of the period. The third century BC was an age of engineering and techno-logical innovation, much of it once again associated with the court of the Ptolemies at Alexandria. Archimedes himself was probably responsible for the invention of the cylindrical water-screw, a hand-turned device used for lifting water, and thus invaluable in Egyptian irrigation-agriculture, as well as in mine-drainage. The force-pump, a more complex water-lifting device, also seems to have been devised in third-century Alexandria. Probably the single most important mechanical invention of the early Hellenistic period was cogwheel gearing, used for the first time in the third century BC, and rapidly applied to a wide variety of practical devices and gadgets (geared winches, water-clocks, planetaria, the hodometer). One of the few surviving products of Hellenistic engineering is the so-called Antikythera mechanism, an elaborate geared instrument recovered from a shipwreck off the coast of the Peloponnese, designed to calculate the movement of astronomical bodies (see Figure 10). In its precision engineering and technical complexity (thirty miniature interlocking gear-wheels of between fifteen and 223 teeth each), the Antikythera mechanism has no parallel in European technology before the Early Modern period.

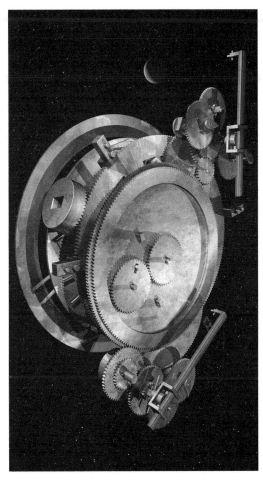

Figure 10 A modern reconstruction of part of the gearing of the bronze 'Antikythera mechanism', a sophisticated astronomical instrument of the second century BC.

Right-angle gearing enabled the development of one of the great triumphs of Greek and Roman technology, the vertical watermill. Although the watermill did not come into widespread industrial use until the Roman Imperial period, recent research has convincingly pushed its invention back to the 240s BC. The water-driven grain mill was a truly Promethean leap forward, substituting water-power for human and animal muscle in one of the central productive technologies of any agrarian society (the milling of grain into flour). A verse epigram of the first century BC, attributed to Antipater of Thessalonice, is one of the most eerie texts to survive from classical antiquity, breathing the spirit of the Industrial Revolution almost two millennia before the event:

> Rest your mill-turning hands, you maidens who grind; sleep on,
>> Even when the cock-crow announces the dawn;
> For Demeter has assigned the toil of your hands to the
>> water-nymphs,
>> Who now leap on the very edge of the wheel,
> And whirl the axle which, with its revolving cogs,
>> Turns the hollow weight of the Nisyrean millstones.
> We taste again the golden age of old, as we learn to feast
>> On the works of Demeter [i.e. cereals], free from human labour.

The Ptolemaic kings—particularly Ptolemy II Philadelphus—stand out among Hellenistic rulers as willing financiers and patrons of this great wave of mathematical, scientific and technological research. No doubt, they had good practical reasons for encouraging technological innovation: one of the few research projects specifically attributed to Ptolemaic royal initiative was intended to increase the power and range of torsion artillery. But let us not be churlish. No independent Greek city-state could have produced an object like the Antikythera mechanism. For a crucial few decades in the third century BC, the scientists of Ptolemaic Alexandria were encouraged to imagine the unimaginable, and were given the resources to put it into practice.

Poetry and Literary Scholarship

One of the more unexpected features of Alexandrian scholarship is the broad area of overlap between what we now call the humanities and the sciences (a distinction that did not exist in antiquity). Eratosthenes himself was an accomplished poet; what is more, at least some of his poetry was concerned with the subject-matter of the natural sciences. The only one of Eratosthenes' works to survive complete is a short mathematical treatise, addressed to King Ptolemy III Euergetes (reigned 246–221 BC), on the problem of the duplication of the cube—that is to say, how to calculate the linear measurements of a solid whose volume is double that of a given solid of like proportions. After a sober mathematical exposition of the problem, Eratosthenes concludes his work with an eighteen-line verse epigram:

Friend, if you intend to fashion a double-sized cube from a smaller one,
Or successfully to metamorphose any solid form into another,

Then here is your answer, even if you wish to measure
  In this way a cattle-byre, or corn-pit, or the broad body
Of a hollow well: you must catch between two rulers
  Two means with their extreme ends converging.
Do not seek the impractical business of Archytas' cylinders,
  Nor to cut the cone in the triads of Menaechmus,
Nor whatever shape of curved lines is found
  In the writings of god-fearing Eudoxus.
For through my tables you will easily be able to construct
  Innumerable mean proportionals, starting from a small base.
Blessed Ptolemy [III], father of the same youthful vigour as your son,
  You have bestowed all that is dear both to the Muses
And to monarchs. As for the future, heavenly Zeus,
  May he [*i.e.* Ptolemy IV] also obtain the royal sceptre from your hand.
And may all this come to pass, and let him who looks on this dedication say:
  This is the work of Eratosthenes of Cyrene.

Eratosthenes here offers a crisp summary of the whole treatise. He outlines his main conclusions, indicates their practical real-world applications (a kind of Ptolemaic Impact Assessment), castigates earlier writings on the subject, and gives fulsome thanks to the monarch whose patronage has allowed him to conduct his research. What is startling is that he chooses to present this report in impeccable elegiac verse. This was not just an act of personal whimsy. Archimedes' *Cattle Problem*—a fiendishly difficult mathematical puzzle, the full solution to which was not obtained until 1965—similarly takes the form of a poem of twenty-two elegiac couplets.

These poems are not doggerel: peculiar though it appears to us, mathematicians like Archimedes and Eratosthenes took as much care over the 'literary' presentation of their work as they did over the problems and solutions themselves.

Self-evidently, no hard dividing line can be drawn between Alexandrian science and Alexandrian poetry. Indeed, one of the defining features of Hellenistic poetry is precisely its erudite and technical character. In antiquity, the most widely read and admired Hellenistic verse text was Aratus' *Phaenomena* ('Visible Signs'), composed at Antigonus Gonatas' Macedonian court in the mid-third century BC. This long poem, on constellations and weather-signs, falls into a long Greek tradition of 'didactic' or 'educative' poetry, going back to the *Works and Days* of the Boeotian poet Hesiod (*c.* 700 BC). What distinguishes the *Phaenomena* from earlier didactic poems is Aratus' bravura translation of technical geometric astronomy into the language of poetry. The first two-thirds of the *Phaenomena* are an ingenious poetic guide to the night sky, based on an earlier prose work by the astronomer Eudoxus of Cnidus; the final third explains how to predict weather conditions from natural phenomena (birds, clouds, the appearance of the moon). Aratus' poem was later rendered into Latin by both Cicero and Ovid; a large part of the first book of Virgil's *Georgics* is based on Aratus, and the poem was even quoted by the Apostle Paul in his sermon on the Areopagus (Acts 17:28).

The scientific mindset can be clearly seen in the more traditionally 'humanistic' activities of scholars associated with the Alexandrian Museum. In the early third century BC, as contemporary papyrus fragments show, Homer's *Iliad* and *Odyssey* were circulating in a wide variety of different texts, littered with extra lines, omissions, and variant readings. A whole series of Alexandrian scholars, beginning with Zenodotus of Ephesus in the second quarter of the third century, dedicated themselves to the careful editing and critical explication of the Homeric text. This process culminated in the full textual edition and commentary on the *Iliad* and *Odyssey* composed around 150 BC by Aristarchus of Samos. The impact of this great work was immediate and final: textual variants abruptly disappear from Homeric papyri of the later second century BC, and the text of Homer that has come down to us in medieval manuscripts is essentially the one established by Aristarchus. This critical approach was soon extended to other 'classic' literary texts (indeed, the very category of the 'classic' was an invention of Museum scholars): Eratosthenes himself wrote a huge twelve-volume work *On Old Comedy*, in which he studied rare vocabulary and dialect forms in the fifth-century Attic comedies of Aristophanes and his contemporaries. Classification, tabulation and critical analysis of the Greek literary heritage was one of the chief aims of Alexandrian scholarship. Something of the tone and method of this vast encyclopedic project can be gained from a list (preserved in a medieval Greek lexicon, the *Suda*) of the major works of the third-century poet and scholar Callimachus of Cyrene, the alleged author of more than 800 books in total:

Here are some of the books written by him: the *Arrival of Io*; *Semele*; the *Foundation of Argos*; *Arcadia*; *Glaucus*; the *Hopes*; satyr plays; tragedies; comedies; lyric poems; the *Ibis*, an elaborately obscure and unpleasant poem, against a certain 'Ibis', an enemy of Callimachus—this is in fact Apollonius, who wrote the *Argonautica*; the *Museum*; *Pinakes* ['Tables'] of all those who excelled in every genre of literature, and lists of their works, in 120 volumes; a *Pinax* and account of teachers, listed from the beginning in chronological order; a *Pinax* of words and compounds found in the works of Democritus; the *Names of the Months* in the various tribes and cities; the *Foundations* of islands and cities and their changes of name; *On the Rivers in Europe*; *On the Marvels and Wonders of the Peloponnese and Italy*; *On Changes in the Names of Fish*; *On Winds*; *On Birds*; *On the Rivers of the World*; a *Collection of Wonders* of the entire world, in geographical order.

We might remark on one striking absence from this list. There is no sign that Callimachus ever engaged with the rich history, antiquities, or literature of his adopted homeland, Egypt. Alexandrian literary scholarship was very definitely for—and about—Greeks only.

Beyond Alexandria

The great age of the Alexandrian Museum ended abruptly in 144 BC, when Ptolemy VIII *Kakergetes* ('Malefactor') expelled the greater part of the city's scholarly community, apparently in revenge for their having favoured a dynastic rival. But the Ptolemies were not the only royal patrons of intellectual and cultural activity in the Hellenistic world. We have already seen that Aratus' *Phaenomena* was composed at the Macedonian court of Antigonus Gonatas; at Syracuse, Hieron II (reigned *c.* 269–215 BC) enjoyed the services of Archimedes and—for at least part of his career—the bucolic poet Theocritus. Most enthusiastic of all were the Attalid dynasty of Pergamon in north-west Asia Minor, who, from the late third century onwards, built up a royal library to rival that of Alexandria. In the absence of a native supply of papyrus, most of the books in the Pergamene library were written on leather 'parchment': the English word is a distant descendant of the adjective 'Pergamene'. The most important scholar attached to the Pergamene library was Crates of Mallos, the proponent—in stark contrast to his more sober Alexandrian contemporaries—of fanciful allegorical interpretations of the Homeric poems.

Perhaps surprisingly, the scholars of the Alexandrian Museum paid little attention to philosophy. In this field—and in this field alone—the city of Athens maintained its pre-eminence in the Greek world right down through the Hellenistic period and beyond. By the late fourth century, two major Athenian 'schools' of philosophy were already in existence, Plato's Academy and Aristotle's Lyceum (also known as the Peripatetic school, from the *peripatos* or 'walkway' of the Lyceum in which Aristotle taught). In the last decade of the fourth century, two heterodox philosophers, Epicurus of Samos and Zeno of Citium, settled at Athens. The philosophical traditions founded by these two men, Epicureanism and Stoicism (named after the Painted Stoa at Athens, where Zeno taught), proved astonishingly fertile and long-lived. Most significant Roman philosophical writing is either Epicurean (Lucretius, Philodemus) or Stoic (Seneca, Epictetus, Marcus Aurelius) in inspiration.

Very little is known of the structure of the four chief philosophical 'schools' of Hellenistic Athens. They were not formal institutions like the Alexandrian Museum, and none depended on state support. Probably we should think of loose communities of teachers and adherents, much as we might speak today of a 'school' of Wittgenstein or Foucault. It is striking how few of the significant figures of Hellenistic philosophy were natives of Athens. Young men from across the Greek world gravitated to Athens for a philosophical training, where they were taught, for the most part, by non-Athenians. The Athenian state was quick to recognize the benefits it could reap from this steady influx of bright young things. In 155 BC, Rome imposed a crippling fine on Athens for plundering the neighbouring town of Oropus, and the Athenians were compelled to dispatch an embassy to Rome to beg for a reduction in the size of the fine. The three chosen ambassadors were all non-Athenians, the heads of the three main philosophical schools of the day: the Academic Carneades of Cyrene, the Peripatetic Critolaus of Phaselis, and the Stoic Diogenes of Seleucia.

Perhaps the single most distinctive feature of Hellenistic philosophy is its turn away from politics and political theory towards the cultivation and perfection of the individual. The political planning of Plato's *Republic* and Aristotle's *Politics* had no Hellenistic sequels. Instead, the Epicureans and Stoics (and other Hellenistic schools of thought, the Cynics and Sceptics) understood the task of philosophy to be the therapeutic treatment of the individual soul. Epicureans and Stoics offered different paths to the relief of human misery: for an Epicurean, the only intrinsic good lies in tranquillity and the absence of pain, which can be achieved by the surgical extirpation of bad habits and false desires; for a Stoic, the consistent and dogged application of rational thought and self-scrutiny would gradually lead the student to a realm of moral freedom and dignity. Epicureanism purported to offer a one-off, self-contained medical short-cut to the good life; Stoicism an ongoing habit of thought which would get you there in the end.

Neither system concerned itself much with human communities outside the narrow circle of its own devotees. The individual Stoic, or so it was believed, would necessarily come to understand his true status as a 'citizen of the world' (*kosmou politēs*). Hence if only enough people could be persuaded to accept the doctrines of Stoicism, a rational, egalitarian, moral society would inevitably be the result. When it came to the actually existing laws and institutions of the Hellenistic city-states and kingdoms, the Epicurean and the Stoic had little to offer: they could look down on the messy compromises and injustices of Hellenistic politics with serene superiority. It is all too easy to understand how Stoicism became, under the Roman empire, the favoured doctrine of the well-off senatorial elite.

Ptolemy II of Egypt, Antigonus Gonatas of Macedon, Magas of Cyrene, and Alexander II of Epirus.

What dealings Ashoka might have had with the remote principalities of Cyrene and Epirus, heaven only knows. Still, his grasp of the political geography of the eastern Mediterranean is impressive. The Indian encounter with Greece was one with momentous consequences for both sides: the extraordinary flowering of Gandharan Buddhist art (a hybrid of Greek and Indian styles) is only the most obvious example of the rich cultural traffic between the sub-continent and the Greek civilizations of Asia. It is salutary to recall that the longest Greek inscription to survive from the Hellenistic Far East is an edict authored by Ashoka himself, cut into a rock-face at modern Kandahar (ancient Alexandria in Arachosia), describing the king's Buddhist philosophy in elaborate and impeccable Greek prose.

The inscriptions of Ashoka give us a sense of the almost unimaginable scale of the Hellenistic world—the world which was being mapped and described at precisely this date (the mid-third century BC) by Eratosthenes at the Alexandrian Museum, 3,350 miles to the west of Ashoka's capital at Pataliputra. In this chapter, we will travel to the outermost limits of Hellenistic civilization, where the Graeco-Macedonian societies of the Mediterranean and western Asia rubbed shoulders with sophisticated and powerful non-Greek neighbours. In the Far East, we will visit the extraordinary city of Aï Khanoum, a Greek city on the banks of the Oxus in north-east Afghanistan, with its Greek theatre, Mesopotamian-style temple and vast mud-brick palace. To the south, we will follow the great sea-captain Eudoxus of Cyzicus on his journey of exploration across the Southern Ocean, forging the first direct link between Ptolemaic Egypt and the Indian subcontinent. To the north, we will visit Olbia in southern Ukraine, a Greek city under constant pressure from Scythian steppe nomads, and in the far west, we will examine the Villa of the Papyri at Herculaneum, the luxury dwelling of a Roman aristocrat of the mid-first century BC.

East: Aristotle in the Hindu Kush

A hundred and thirty miles east of the Afghan city of Mazar-i-Sharif, on the left bank of the River Oxus, lie the ruins of an ancient city, today known as Aï Khanoum ('Lady Moon' in Uzbek). Partially excavated by a French team between 1964 and 1978, Aï Khanoum has a special place in the heart of any Hellenistic historian. This is the only Hellenistic Greek city excavated anywhere east of Mesopotamia: most of what we think we know about the history of the Greeks in the Far East comes from this one remarkable site.

The town lies on a roughly triangular site in the angle between the Oxus river (the modern Amu Darya) and its southern tributary, the Kokcha. It was a big place: the main road through the city runs as straight as an arrow for a little over a mile, and the landward flank of the town was defended by a colossal set of mud-brick fortifications, a good mile and a half in length (see Figure 11). The city seems to have been founded by Seleucus I in the years around 300 BC, within a generation or so of Alexander the Great's conquest of Afghanistan. Its history was cruelly brief: in 145 BC, give

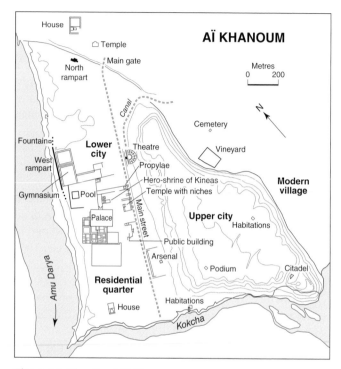

Figure 11 The site of Aï Khanoum.

or take a few years, Aï Khanoum was sacked (it is not clear by whom), and never subsequently reoccupied.

Seleucus was not the first to see the potential of this magnificent site. The fertile valley of the Oxus, ancient Bactria, had been one of the wealthiest provinces of the Achaemenid Persian empire. Already under the Achaemenids,

Aï Khanoum seems to have served as an administrative centre for upper Bactria; the great Hellenistic palace-complex at Aï Khanoum, laid out on a different orientation from the rest of the city, probably lies on top of an Achaemenid-era palace. But the Hellenistic city was planned on a far larger scale than its putative Achaemenid predecessor. Monumental Greek-style public buildings—a theatre, a colossal gymnasium, an arsenal—were strung out along the main road through the town. The main residential district (at the far western corner of the site) was made up of very large private houses, equipped with private bathrooms in Greek style. At the centre of the town stood a hero-shrine to the city's founder, Kineas of Thessaly; it was here, in the mausoleum of Kineas, that the maxims of the Seven Sages of Greece, brought from the Delphic sanctuary of Apollo, were inscribed on stone by the travelling philosopher Clearchus of Soli (Chapter 1).

At first glance, Aï Khanoum looks like a Greek city transplanted from the Aegean and dropped into the heart of central Asia. With the exception of a single scrap of Aramaic on a potsherd, every written document from Aï Khanoum is in the Greek language; papyrus and parchment fragments from the palace treasury preserve scraps of a lost philosophical work by Aristotle, and what appears to be a Classical Greek tragic drama. The public buildings of Aï Khanoum were adorned with Corinthian columns, pebble mosaic floors, and Greek terracotta antefixes. It is tempting to think of Aï Khanoum as a kind of colonial 'Little Hellas' on the Oxus.

Tempting, but wrong. The fact that Aï Khanoum had a Greek-style theatre and a Greek-style gymnasium does not, in itself, prove anything very much about the ethnicity of the people who used these buildings, or what they used them for. There is little sign that Aï Khanoum was ever organized as a Greek *polis*: no inscribed civic decrees were found at the site, and the city lacks many of the characteristic buildings of Greek public life (no council-house, *prytaneion*, or *agora*). The main temple at Aï Khanoum (the 'Temple with Indented Niches'), dedicated to an unknown deity, was a squat Mesopotamian-style structure of mudbrick, quite unlike any Greek cult building known to us. The enormous palace that looms over the central part of the town finds its closest parallels in the Achaemenid world, and seems to have functioned both as the ceremonial seat of a local dynast or governor and as a centre of storage and redistribution for valuable goods (unworked blocks of lapis lazuli, mined in the mountains north-east of Aï Khanoum, were found in the palace treasury).

In the light of all this, one starts to wonder whether the inhabitants of Aï Khanoum were even Greek. Well, maybe they were, and maybe they weren't—it all depends on what we think 'Greek' means. At least some of the original settlers, like Kineas the Thessalian, were immigrants from the Aegean. But intermarriage between Greeks and Bactrians was clearly common enough: the Seleucid king Antiochus I was himself the product of a union between the Macedonian Seleucus and a Sogdian (Uzbek) princess named Apame. Even those locals who did not end up marrying into Greek families must have had strong incentives to take on Greek names, learn the Greek language, and adopt at least some Greek cultural practices. There is certainly no sign of any ethnically based *apartheid* at Aï Khanoum: second-century documents from the palace treasury show people with Greek, Iranian, and Bactrian personal names working alongside one another. The people of Aï Khanoum were keen to 'act Greek' in some contexts (the theatre, the gymnasium), but were equally happy to 'act Bactrian' in others (public religion, perhaps also the political sphere). Their 'real' ethnicity may simply not have been all that important.

The dividing line between Greek and non-Greek at Aï Khanoum was clearly blurry at best. The same seems to have been true elsewhere in Bactria. A hundred miles downstream from Aï Khanoum, at a place called Takht-i Sangin, lie the ruins of an Iranian-style temple of Hellenistic date, where men with Bactrian names made Greek-style offerings to the local river-god Oxus. A certain Atrosokes set up a little bronze figurine depicting the mythological Greek satyr Marsyas, accompanied by a short Greek-language inscription ('Atrosokes dedicated this to Oxus, in fulfilment of a vow': see Figure 12). Another Greek inscription from this temple, first published in 2008, is an even richer cross-cultural cocktail: 'Iromois, son of Nemiskos, *molrpalres*, dedicated to Oxus a bronze cauldron weighing seven talents, in accordance with a vow'. The dedication itself, aside from a few oddities of spelling, is perfectly Greek in form. But the dedicator carries an Iranian name, 'Iromois'; his father's name, 'Nemiskos', could be of either Greek or Kushan origin; and '*molrpalres*' is a Bactrian word apparently meaning 'keeper of the seal'. This little text is a beautiful illustration of the new, hybrid 'Graeco-Bactrian' culture of the Hellenistic Far

Figure 12 Atrosokes' dedication to the Oxus.

East: strange exchanges, old gods worshipped in new ways, and new settlers gradually becoming indistinguishable from locals.

Tragically, we are unlikely ever to learn much more about the encounter between Greeks and Bactrians at Aï Khanoum. In recent years, like many other archaeological sites in Afghanistan, Iraq, and Syria, Aï Khanoum has been stripped bare by local treasure-hunters: today the site has been reduced to a desolate moonscape, pockmarked with craters. The flood of Hellenistic artefacts from Bactria—inscriptions, coins, sculptures, jewellery—onto the international antiquities market since 2002 tells its own, melancholy story.

South: Argonauts of the Monsoon

Until the late fourth century BC, the Greeks were unaware of the existence of the Indian Ocean. The Red Sea and the Persian Gulf were traditionally considered to be inland seas. When Alexander the Great crossed into India in 326 BC, he still believed that the Indus river and the Nile were connected, a hypothesis which seemed briefly to be confirmed by the presence in the Indus of crocodiles and lotus-plants (previously thought to be unique to the Nile). The existence of a great ocean at the mouth of the Indus river came as a rude shock to Alexander and his men. Alexander's admiral Nearchus was sent west to explore the sea-route along the Baluchistan coast in 325 BC; he brought back strange tales of monstrous sea-creatures out in the deep, which blew water upwards from the sea as if from a waterspout.

Nearchus' sea-journey from the Indus to the mouth of the Euphrates revealed a vast new southern maritime world to the Hellenistic Greeks. In the third and second centuries BC, the Persian Gulf was administered by a Seleucid royal governor of 'Tylos [Bahrain] and the Islands', based at a remote Greek colonial outpost at Qalat al-Bahrain; the Seleucid monarchs enjoyed a profitable trading relationship with the great caravan city of Gerrha (modern Thaj) in the east Arabian desert. But there is little sign that the Seleucids extended their reach beyond the Oman peninsula. The opening up of the Indian Ocean was the result of a single chance encounter 200 years after Nearchus' pioneering voyage.

Around 120 BC, late in the reign of Ptolemy VIII *Physkon* ('Fatso'), a man by the name of Eudoxus arrived in Egypt. Eudoxus was an ambassador for his home city of Cyzicus in north-west Turkey, and had been dispatched to Alexandria to announce the imminent celebration of a major international festival at Cyzicus. The Greek historian Posidonius takes up the story:

> Eudoxus fell in with the king and his court, and accompanied them on journeys up the Nile, being as he was a man naturally curious about strange places, and already widely travelled. It happened that a certain Indian was brought to the king by the garrison of the Red Sea, who said that they had found him alone, shipwrecked and half-dead; who he was, and where he came from, they did not know, since they did not understand his language. The king handed him

over to people to teach him Greek, and once he had learned the language, he explained that he had lost his way while sailing from India. All his shipmates had died of hunger, and he alone had reached Egypt safely. He was taken at his word, and he promised to guide a crew chosen by the king on the sea-route to India. Eudoxus was one of the men selected.

What this anonymous Indian brought to the Hellenistic world was knowledge of the monsoon winds. Every year, from March to September, the south-west monsoon blows steadily from Somalia to India; in winter, the winds change direction, and a sailing boat can travel directly across the open ocean from the sub-continent to the mouth of the Red Sea. Eudoxus and his crew were the first Greeks to sail to India by this route; a year later he returned to Egypt with a boat groaning with perfumes and precious stones. A couple of years later, in 116 or 115 BC, Eudoxus set out a second time for India, this time with a larger expedition. On his return journey, the winds blew him off course, and he made landfall south of the Horn of Africa, somewhere on the Somali coast:

> Driven ashore at this remote place, Eudoxus won over the locals by giving them bread, wine, and dried figs, things that they had never come across before; in return they gave him fresh water and the services of their pilots. He compiled a list of some of the local words. Here, too, he came across the wooden prow of a wrecked ship, with a horse carved on it. He learned that this was the shipwreck of some sailors who had come from the west, and he took the prow with him when he set sail for home.

This, so far as we know, was the last voyage undertaken by Eudoxus across the Indian Ocean. The trading route that he discovered was richly exploited by the later Ptolemies, and subsequently by the Romans: Roman coins have been found in vast numbers in southern India and Sri Lanka, and Roman ports on the Red Sea received huge cargoes of Indian pepper, ivory, spices, and luxury fabrics. Eudoxus himself seems to have been haunted by the carved wooden horse on the prow from the Somali coast. The sea-captains of Alexandria recognized the horse-prow as coming from one of the small fishing-boats of Gadeira (modern Cadiz, west of Gibraltar), which plied their trade up and down the Atlantic seaboard. Eudoxus believed—rightly or wrongly—that one of these boats had wandered too far south, and ended up making its way round the Cape of Good Hope to Somalia.

In the end, Eudoxus sold all his possessions to raise the money for an expedition down the West African coast. At his first attempt, he sailed south beyond the Canary Islands (which he sighted, but did not explore), 'until he met with people who spoke some of the same words as he had noted down previously'. It is hard to believe that the natives of—let us say—Mauretania really spoke the same language as the inhabitants of ancient Somalia, but this was enough to convince Eudoxus that a West African passage to India was feasible. Perhaps around 100 BC, he set out with two fine ships on a second journey towards the Cape, carrying on board agricultural tools, seeds, and carpenters, in case they needed to pass the winter in the Canaries or still more distant African lands. He was never heard of again.

North: Protogenes and Saitaphernes

In the sixth century BC, traders from the Ionian Greek city of Miletus founded a small trading post called Olbia at the mouth of the modern River Bug (ancient Hypanis), 50 miles east of Odessa on the northern Black Sea coast. Olbia rapidly grew into one of the most prosperous Greek settlements in the Black Sea, enjoying a flourishing trade in furs, slaves, and livestock with the various steppe peoples to the north, known to the Greeks as 'Scythians'. We cannot trace the history of relations between the Olbian Greeks and the Scythians in any detail, although the spectacular 'Graeco-Scythian' metalwork found in fourth-century Scythian tombs across Ukraine shows the intense and fertile cultural interchange between the two peoples. Herodotus preserves a bizarre story about the Scythian king Scyles, a steppe chieftain of the mid-fifth century BC. Scyles is said to have owned a spacious house in Olbia, surrounded by statues of sphinxes and griffins, which he used to visit for the occasional holiday *à la grecque*, dressing in Greek clothes and worshipping the Greek gods of Olbia like any ordinary citizen; after a few weeks, he would resume his normal Scythian dress, and return to his kingdom in the steppe.

A welcome shaft of light is shed on Graeco-Scythian relations by a long Hellenistic inscription from Olbia, dating to the years around 200 BC. This text is a decree in honour of a wealthy civic benefactor by the name of Protogenes, who repeatedly bailed his city out with cash gifts and loans in the face of a rolling series of crises (grain-shortages, spiralling private and public debt, short-term liquidity shortfalls). The gradual emergence across the Greek world of figures like Protogenes—what we might call 'career benefactors', super-rich individuals who acted as financial guardians of their fellow-citizens in return for lavish public honours—is a key feature of the later Hellenistic period, which we will return to in Chapter 6.

What is distinctive about the situation at Olbia (and presumably the whole northern Black Sea region) is the steady financial pressure exercised by the neighbouring Scythians of the steppe, and in particular by a tribe known as the Saioi. The Saioi were divided into several different minor chiefdoms, ruled over by men called *skēptouchoi*, 'sceptre-bearers'; the most important chieftain, perhaps a kind of overall tribal king, was a certain Saitaphernes. Saitaphernes and other Scythian dynasts would periodically come downstream along the Hypanis river to the borders of Olbian territory, and request 'gifts' from the people of Olbia. These 'gifts' conventionally took the form of large bags full of gold coins: on more than one occasion, the Olbians found themselves unable to summon up the necessary cash, and called on Protogenes to help out:

> When King Saitaphernes arrived at Kankytos and demanded the gifts due for his passage, and the public treasury was exhausted, Protogenes was called upon by the people and gave 400 gold pieces...[Some time later], when the Saioi came by to receive their gifts, the people were unable to satisfy them, and called on Protogenes to help out in this crisis; he came forward and promised 400 gold pieces. When he was elected as one of the city's Nine magistrates, he lent 1,500 gold pieces to be repaid from the city's future revenues,

out of which several *skēptouchoi* were placated in good time, and several gifts were gainfully provided to the King.

It would be quite wrong to think of these payments from Olbia to the Saioi as simple extortion, or (more generously) as a semi-formal 'Scythian tribute'. In fact, 'gift' is precisely the right word for these occasional exchanges. For the Saioi, receiving periodic ritualized gifts from the Olbians was an indication of mutual respect and goodwill: regular gift-exchange symbolized and confirmed the ongoing friendship between the two parties. As a result, Saitaphernes seems to have placed a far higher premium than the Olbians did on the correct performance of the regular 'gift-giving' ceremony. On one occasion, the relationship between Saitaphernes and Olbia seems to have broken down altogether, as a result of some mortal offence inadvertently committed in the transfer of gifts:

> When King Saitaphernes arrived on the far side of the river to receive his gifts, the magistrates called an assembly, reported on the king's arrival, and said that the city's revenues were exhausted; Protogenes came forward and gave 900 gold pieces. But when the ambassadors, Protogenes and Aristocrates, took the money and met with the king, the king rejected the gifts, flew into a rage, and broke up his camp . . .

The nature of the insult is somewhat unclear; indeed, the Olbians themselves may not have understood exactly what they had done wrong.

The second half of the decree in honour of Protogenes describes a very different, and far more perilous state of affairs. As a result of Olbia's good relationships with Saitaphernes and the Saioi, the city was partially unwalled, and those stretches of fortification that did exist had been left to fall into ruins. But rumours began to trickle in that a new threat was looming from the steppe:

> Deserters started bringing in reports that the Galatians and the Skiroi had made an alliance, that a large force had been gathered, and that it would be here when winter came. They also reported that the Thisarnatai, Scythians and Sauadaratai were eager to seize the fort (i.e. the city of Olbia), since they too were similarly frightened of the savagery of the Galatians. Because of this, many people fell into despair, and started preparing to abandon the city. At the same time, the city also suffered many losses in its rural territory: the entire slave population had taken to its heels, as had the half-Greeks who inhabit the land beyond the hills, no fewer than 1,500 in number, who had fought as our allies in the city during the previous war; many of the resident foreigners had also fled, as had no small number of the citizens.

The migration eastwards of a band of Galatian Celts from the lower Danube basin has violently upset the equilibrium between Greek Olbia and its Scythian neighbours. The nearby Scythian tribes are now, we are told, planning on seizing Olbia themselves, in order to have a fortified base against the imminent Galatian invasion. The decree goes on to describe how Protogenes put up the money for a rapid repair-job on the wall-circuit. We do not know what actually happened that baleful winter at Olbia; the fact that the decree for Protogenes survives at all may indicate that the defence of the city, both against the Galatians and against the Olbians' former Scythian allies, was successful.

Finally, we would love to know more about the mysterious 'half-Greeks' (*mixellēnes*) living in the hinterland of Olbia. That the territory of Olbia was partly worked by a rural slave population comes as little surprise: the same was true of many, if not most, Greek cities of the Hellenistic world. It is far more interesting to find a group defined by their mixed racial origin, who appear to live in a distinct part of Olbian territory ('the land beyond the hills'). Clearly these rural 'half-Greeks' were not citizens of Olbia, and their loyalty to the Olbians was intermittent at best. Whether the Olbians had their own formal Nuremberg Laws, we cannot say; at the very least, on this particular fringe of the Hellenistic world, 'real' Greeks were especially keen to distinguish themselves from half-Scythian *Mischlinge*.

West: The Villa of the Papyri

Among the sites on the Bay of Naples buried under volcanic material by the eruption of Mount Vesuvius in AD 79 was a large private house, overlooking the seashore on the northwest outskirts of the Roman town of Herculaneum. Partially excavated in the 1750s and 1760s, the house quickly became famous for its superb collection of bronze and marble sculptures (some eighty-five pieces in total, now on display in the Naples Archaeological Museum), and, above all, for more than 1,000 carbonized papyrus-rolls, most of them discovered in a small 'library' in the main house.

The house—conventionally known as the Villa of the Papyri—seems to have been built shortly after 50 BC (see Figure 13). It was a huge, sprawling structure, around

250 x 80 metres (20,000m^2). The main house consisted of a sumptuous complex of rooms on several levels, grouped around an atrium; a long formal garden, enclosed by colonnades on all four sides ('peristyle'), extended north-west from the main residence. The house's owner clearly belonged to the uppermost crust of Roman society. It is, then, a surprise to find that almost all of the papyrus-rolls unearthed in the Villa were in Greek rather than Latin. Most of the papyri contain highly specialized works of Epicurean philosophy, dominated by the writings of a minor Epicurean thinker by the name of Philodemus of Gadara (*c.* 110–40 BC). Indeed, the collection looks very much like it might have been Philodemus' own personal library, no doubt bequeathed to the owner of the Villa of the Papyri on his death. Many of Philodemus' works were dedicated to his wealthy Roman patron, a nobleman called Lucius Calpurnius Piso Caesonianus, father-in-law to Julius Caesar. It is a reasonable guess—though no more than that—that the Villa of the Papyri served as the country home of the family of the Calpurnii Pisones.

Of all the various encounters between Greeks and non-Greeks in the Hellenistic world, none was more fertile (and complex) than the love-affair between Roman Italy and the Greek East in the second and first centuries BC. Greeks and Italians had been in contact with one another for a long time. Since the eighth century BC, southern Italy and Sicily had been dotted with Greek colonies; Naples itself (ancient Neapolis), a mere 6 miles north-west of Herculaneum, was a Greek settlement dating back to the sixth century. It is hardly surprising that the private houses of Late Republican

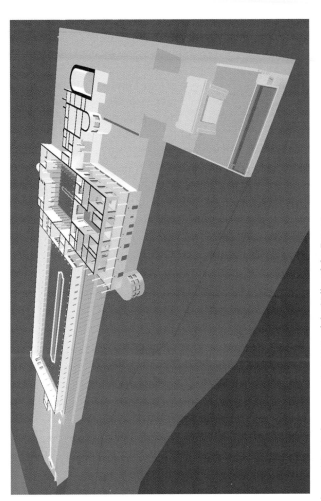

Figure 13 Modern reconstruction of the Villa of the Papyri.

Herculaneum or Pompeii should show signs of Greek influence. But the 'Hellenization' of the non-Greek parts of Italy (Rome included) does seem to have accelerated sharply after Rome's first conquests in the Hellenistic East from the 220s onwards. Second-century Italy was flooded with war-booty from the Greek East (sculptures, paintings, metalwork). The first marble building in the city of Rome, the temple of Jupiter Stator in the Campus Martius, was dedicated by the Roman general Q. Caecilius Metellus to commemorate his victory over the Macedonian pretender Andriskos in 148 BC; it is telling—and perhaps a shade ironic—that Metellus chose to have it designed by a Greek architect.

For the Roman aristocratic elite, the adoption of Greek material culture became a symbol of their membership of the 'conquering class'. The Villa of the Papyri is one of our best examples of this ostentatiously Hellenized elite culture in Late Republican Italy. The physical form of the house was designed to evoke the public architecture of contemporary Greek cities. The huge peristyle garden imitates the colonnaded courtyards of Greek gymnasia, the chief educational and leisure establishments of Hellenistic cities in the East. Roman aristocrats went so far as to name parts of their houses after Greek public buildings: Cicero referred to the peristyle garden of his villa at Tusculum as his 'gymnasium', 'palaestra', or even 'Academy' (after Plato's Academy at Athens). If, as some historians suspect, Philodemus in fact spent his final years living at the Villa of the Papyri, then the mock-gymnasium attached to the villa would even have had its own resident Greek philosopher ambling through its elegant porticos.

The sculptural décor of the Villa of the Papyri gives a vivid picture of the cultural aspirations of the Late Republican Roman elite. Almost all of the sculptures are reproductions of earlier Greek statues or portrait busts, depicting Greek gods and goddesses, philosophers, Hellenistic kings, and athletes. Several of the smaller rooms in the house were decorated with miniature 'table-top' bronze portrait busts of Greek philosophers, with members of the Epicurean school particularly well-represented. Copies of famous Greek masterpieces included a life-size bronze reproduction of the head of Polycleitus' *Doryphorus* and a striding Panathenaic Athena in marble. An over-life-size statue of the fourth-century Athenian orator Aeschines stood overlooking the peristyle garden, which was also dotted with marble portrait busts of early Hellenistic kings and dynasts (Demetrius Poliorcetes, Philetaerus of Pergamon, Pyrrhus of Epirus, and others).

Much ingenuity has been dedicated to analysing the sculptural 'programme' of the Villa of the Papyri. Was the owner of the villa drawing symbolic analogies between his own political career and the lives of famous Greek orators and Hellenistic kings (rhetorical success, enlightened statesmanship, military virtue)? Are the various portrait busts meant to evoke the double life of the Roman aristocrat—a public life of oratory, politics, and war, and a private existence dedicated to philosophy and civilized leisure? Perhaps; but this may be reading too much into what is, in truth, a pretty miscellaneous selection. We have a revealing sequence of letters sent by Cicero to his friend Atticus (then resident at Athens), asking him, in essence, to pick up any old bits of Greek sculpture he can find at a good price, in order to decorate the public spaces of Cicero's own villa at Tusculum. Even a highly civilized Roman like Cicero was not too fussed about the details of his garden furniture, so long as the whole collection gave off a general aura of Hellenic sophistication. And it is worth recalling that the Villa of the Papyri did also include sculptures on somewhat less elevated themes. In the most prominent spot of all, at the far end of the peristyle from the main house, stood an explicit (and technically superb) marble sculpture of a satyr raping a she-goat—presumably no symbolic analogies here.

Either way, the Villa of the Papyri is a symbol of a way of life that is simply unimaginable anywhere east of the Adriatic. Private patronage of intellectuals, of the kind that we can infer for Calpurnius Piso and Philodemus, was unknown in the Hellenistic Greek world; not even a Macedonian king would have been so boorish as to purchase a philosopher as his own personal status-symbol. For all the Romans' sententious moralizing about Hellenic luxury, there are no private houses (and not many royal palaces) on the scale of the Villa of the Papyri anywhere in the Hellenistic East. The very idea of a private collection of Greek art—bronze and marble ersatz sculptures in a mish-mash of styles, based on originals dating from the sixth down to the second century BC—has no real Hellenistic parallels. To a Greek of the second or first century BC, the Romans, despite all their enthusiasm for Epicurean philosophy, must have seemed quite as strange and unfamiliar as any Bactrian or Scythian nomad.

Priene

On the north flank of the Maeander river valley in western Asia Minor, overlooking the flood plain, looms the great rock of Teloneia. Projecting outwards from the Mycale mountain range, Teloneia is a tremendous natural stronghold, protected by steep cliffs to the south and west. At the foot of the rock, just above the Maeander plain, the ground levels off into a descending series of natural terraces, between 130 and 30 metres above the valley floor. Here, in the mid-fourth century BC, was founded the small Greek city of Priene.

Today, Priene lies some 7 miles inland. It was not always so. The Maeander river was famous in antiquity for the vast quantities of silt carried downstream by the river, causing its delta-front to advance westwards faster than any other watercourse in the Mediterranean. Before the fourth century, the Prieneans lived somewhere further up the valley, perhaps near modern Söke, before their access to the sea was choked off by the advancing alluvium of the Maeander delta. Around 350 BC, the Prieneans packed up their possessions and moved 5 or 10 miles south-west to Teloneia, chasing the delta-front downstream. The new city flourished for 250 years or so, before the remorseless forward march of the Maeander alluvium sealed their harbours once again.

As a result, the site of Priene is perhaps our most perfectly preserved example of an ordinary small Hellenistic town. The town was laid out on a green-field site at the very beginning of the Hellenistic period; in the late second century BC, large parts of the town were devastated by fire and never rebuilt, and few significant building works were undertaken after this period. Although Priene continued to be inhabited through the Roman and Byzantine periods, the population seems to have been small, and the physical fabric of the city changed little. Of the 397 known Greek inscriptions from Priene, only sixty-three (16 per cent) can be firmly dated after 50 BC, and most of those sixty-three are short graffiti; of the 200 or so inscribed public documents (civic decrees, honorific statue-bases, letters from Hellenistic kings), only two or three postdate the reign of Augustus. Priene's life as a functioning *polis* largely stopped in the first century BC, leaving us with an exceptionally clear and vivid picture of the Hellenistic city: a true Pompeii of the Hellenistic world.

Planning the City

The town-planners of Priene set to work with geometric precision. The land available for building at the foot of Teloneia was an irregular space of around 15 hectares (37 acres), rising steeply upwards to the north. This space was divided into a rectangular grid-plan, based on precisely regular city-blocks (120 by 160 feet in the local unit of measurement). Most of these blocks were taken up by private housing, usually eight houses per city-block, also of a strictly uniform size ($207m^2$). The city contained around 480 housing units in total, suggesting that the total urban population could have reached 5,000 at the absolute maximum (assuming an upper limit of ten people per household). The rigorous application of this grid-plan on the steeply sloping site meant that many of the streets, particularly those running north-south, had to take the form of stairways, as in modern San Francisco. The main public buildings of the new city were slotted into the grid-plan: the theatre occupies precisely one-and-a-half city-blocks, and the central sanctuary of Athena sprawls over a full three blocks (see Figure 14).

It is hard to say how much we ought to read into the 'egalitarian' planning of Priene's private housing. At one extreme, we could see early Hellenistic Priene as governed by a strong democratic ideology, with its uniform house-sizes reflecting the absolute equality between the *polis'* citizens. In support of this notion, at least some of the fourth-century rural territory of Priene was divided up into agricultural plots of uniform size (50 *schoinoi*, around 5 hectares or 12 acres), suggesting that Prienean citizens might have enjoyed precisely equal shares of both the city's urban and rural space. However, some caution is in order. Uniform housing is found in several Greek cities of the fifth and fourth centuries BC, some of which were certainly governed as oligarchies: the layout of Priene would

Figure 14 The city of Priene.

probably not have struck a fourth-century Greek visitor as distinctively 'democratic'. Many of the citizens of Priene—perhaps the majority—did not live in the city itself, but in the surrounding countryside. That there were no really big houses in the new urban centre might only mean that the rich chose to reside elsewhere. And we should remember that Prienean 'democracy' did not extend to the large serf-like population of non-Greeks living on the city's territory and working its land. The wealth of Priene was built on the backs of a severely oppressed mass of rural 'Plain-dwellers'

(*Pedieis*), the native Carian villagers of south-western Asia Minor, who from time to time rose up in revolt against their Greek masters.

That said, early Hellenistic Priene does give the impression of a prosperous, tight-knit community, with a strong citizen-ethos. The public spaces of the new city were designed with a restrained elegance, and no expense was spared in adorning the major roads and stairways through the town with walls of finely worked blue-grey marble (see Figure 15). Small though it was, the citizen-body of Priene could pull together in impressive fashion at times of crisis. In the mid-270s BC, the

Figure 15 A road-stairway in Priene, with the terrace-wall of the sanctuary of Athena on the right.

territory of Priene was ravaged by a band of Galatian Celts, who had crossed into Asia in 278 BC and spent several years pillaging the rich coastal valleys of western Asia Minor. The city's rural sanctuaries were sacked, the farmhouses in the Maeander plain set on fire, and many of the Greeks living on Prienean territory were put to the sword or taken prisoner. At this point, as we learn from a long honorific decree for a citizen by the name of Sotas, the Prieneans cobbled together a scratch citizen militia to fight the Galatians:

> The *dēmos* of the Prieneans prepared for battle to defend itself against the barbarians who were committing sacrilege against the gods and outrages against the Greeks, sending out paid citizen infantry and [...] horse-breeders, and marched against them in full force; and Sotas gathered around him the bravest of the citizens, along with those of the (non-Greek) rural people who were willing to join in the struggle against the barbarians, and having resolved to rescue the citizens living in the countryside along with their children, wives and possessions, and to bring them safely into the city, he seized the most strategic points in the territory [...] along with his comrades, and rescued many of the citizens who had been taken captive by the Galatians [...], having dared to stand up to their savagery.

The Prieneans were fully able to stand up for themselves in battle. Still, it is worth noting that they could not count on the loyalty of the non-Greek 'Plain-dwellers', only some of whom were willing to join the struggle against the Galatians. Sotas' commando unit was concerned only with the safety of the citizens living in the countryside; the rest of the rural population was left to look after itself. Perhaps most interesting of all is the existence of a distinct class of 'horse-breeders' at Priene, who acted as the city's cavalry in times of war. For all of its egalitarian citizen ethos, Priene clearly still had some kind of blue-blooded aristocracy, which defined itself—as Greek elites had done since time immemorial—by horse-rearing.

Priene and the Kings

The rich coastal valleys of western Asia Minor, densely settled and easy to tax, were a tempting prize for any Hellenistic king or dynast. During the first century after Alexander's death, Priene had to deal with a rapidly changing succession of Macedonian overlords: Antigonus the One-Eyed, Lysimachus of Thrace, and a sequence of warring Ptolemaic and Seleucid kings (whose struggle over south-western Asia Minor spanned the entire third century BC). The Prieneans had to tread carefully, making lavish demonstrations of loyalty to the current power-holder in Asia Minor, while maintaining diplomatic relations with his possible rivals. Fortunately for us, the city recorded its most important dealings with Hellenistic kings (and, later, with the Roman senate) in a kind of monumental public archive, inscribed on the north *anta*-wall of the temple of Athena Polias. The temple was first excavated by the British Society of Dilettanti in 1868/9, and hence much of this invaluable Prienean 'archive wall' is now on display in the British Museum.

The first text to be inscribed on the temple wall was a curt two-line statement: 'King Alexander dedicated the temple to Athena Polias'. We do not know whether Alexander the

Great actually visited Priene during his march through western Asia Minor in 334 BC. (In fact, we do not know whether the new city of Priene existed at all at that point: most likely it was a half-finished building site.) But Alexander was eager to be seen as a liberator to the Greek cities of western Asia Minor from Persian tyranny, and he may well have offered to pay some or all of the costs of the temple in return for having his name prominently displayed at the building's entrance.

Below this two-line dedication the Prieneans inscribed a long extract from an edict of Alexander concerning the city's legal and fiscal status under its new Macedonian rulers. The Prieneans are to be exempt from the *syntaxis* (apparently a kind of military tax payable to the king) and are to enjoy autonomy and freedom, as are all the Greek inhabitants of the city's dependent harbour-town of Naulochon. The city's tax-free territory is defined as a stretch of land lying 'between the sea and the hill of Sandeis'; villages lying outside this zone are to be Alexander's personal possession, and are to pay tribute to him just as they had previously done to the Persian Great King.

Although this edict apparently dates to 334 BC, the Prieneans only got around to inscribing it on their archive wall some fifty years later, in the mid-280s. Why the delay? Most probably Priene's status as a privileged Greek community within the Macedonian Orient, enjoying 'autonomy and freedom' and certain important tax-breaks, had been threatened by one of the successor dynasts (probably Lysimachus). Luckily for the Prieneans, they were able to point to an edict written by the great Alexander himself, guaranteeing their special fiscal status. By the early third century BC, Alexander's decisions on matters like this had acquired the status of law—or at least, a Hellenistic king like Lysimachus could not be seen to be reversing Alexander's original policies towards the city.

In fact, Lysimachus had good reason to view Priene with favour. In 287 BC, Demetrius the Besieger invaded Lysimachus' domains in south-western Asia Minor (Chapter 3), and won over to his cause (among others) the city of Magnesia, Priene's immediate neighbour to the east. The non-Greek serf population of the Maeander plain came over to Demetrius' side, and Priene's territory was ravaged by a coalition of Demetrius' troops, the Magnesians, and the rebel Plain-dwellers. The Prieneans sensibly remained loyal to Lysimachus. A few months later, Demetrius was defeated by Lysimachus' royal army, and the Prieneans were rewarded with a renewal of their favoured status (duly recorded on their archive wall). Priene expressed its gratitude to Lysimachus in what was by now the traditional manner, erecting a colossal bronze statue of the king and establishing a cult in his honour, with annual sacrifices on the king's birthday.

A few years later, the geopolitical context changed again. In spring 281 BC, Lysimachus was defeated and killed by Seleucus I at the battle of Corupedium. The Prieneans promptly set up statues of their new masters, Seleucus and his son Antiochus, in the sanctuary of Athena Polias, probably with an associated ruler-cult; no doubt the existing statue of Lysimachus was quietly retired (no trace of it survives). A Seleucid officer by the name of Larichus then appeared on the scene. Some time in the mid-270s, the Seleucid king Antiochus

I granted Larichus a large private estate on the borders of Prienean territory, worked by slaves rather than serfs. The Prieneans scrambled to win over this powerful new neighbour to their side. They first voted to set up a bronze statue of him in the sanctuary of Athena next to the images of Seleucus and Antiochus, then promptly changed their minds and decided to honour him in an even more visible manner in the main market-place of Priene:

> Instead of the statue previously voted for him, let a bronze equestrian statue of Larichus be erected in the *agora*, and let Larichus enjoy tax-free status for both his livestock and his slaves, as many as he possesses both on his private estates and in the city, so that the *dēmos* should be seen to be repaying Larichus with gratitude worthy of his benefactions.

Precisely what Larichus' benefactions might have been, we cannot say; it is perhaps most likely that he had interceded with the Seleucid king on the Prieneans' behalf. Nor is it clear why the Prieneans decided to honour Larichus with a statue in the *agora* rather than the sanctuary of Athena: perhaps his enormous equestrian statue would have been felt to overshadow the existing statues of the Seleucid kings in the sanctuary. At any rate, the new bronze image of Larichus on horseback must have been one of the most prominent landmarks of mid-third century Priene—a potent symbol of the Prieneans' dependence on the goodwill of the Hellenistic kings and their agents.

In the second century BC the Prieneans continued to solicit the help and support of Hellenistic monarchs with mixed success. A member of the Ariarathid royal dynasty of Cappadocia, one Orophernes, seems to have grown up in exile at Priene. After his seizure of the Cappadocian throne from his half-brother Ariarathes V in 158 BC, Orophernes sent a vast sum of money (400 talents of silver) for safe-keeping in the city. When Orophernes was overthrown the following year, the furious Ariarathes V demanded the money back from the Prieneans, and on their refusal, sent an army to devastate the city's territory. The Prieneans appealed to the Roman senate (their response was duly inscribed on the archive wall of the temple of Athena Polias), and the money eventually made its way back into the hands of Orophernes, now an exile from his kingdom in Seleucid Syria. The Prieneans managed to rebuild their relations with the Cappadocian royal house: we later find them exchanging friendly embassies with King Ariarathes VI (reigned *c.* 130–111 BC), and a vast new stoa on the north side of the Prienean *agora* (the 'Sacred Stoa', constructed around 130 BC) was paid for with Cappadocian royal funds.

The story of Orophernes and Priene has a curious coda. In April 1870, Mr Augustus Oakley Clarke, expatriate manager of the liquorice factory at the nearby Turkish town of Söke, took a day-trip to Priene with his wife and niece. While Clarke was strolling among the ruins of the temple of Athena Polias, near the base of the main cult statue of Athena:

> By chance I found at my feet a coin covered with dirt.
> I washed it, and found it to be silver, and read the name

Orophernes. I then went in search of my wife and niece, who were in the treasury, to inform them of my good luck, and again returned to the base of Athena's pedestal, when the idea struck me that something more might be found under the four intact stones [of the statue-base], so I employed two Greek masons who were working amongst the ruins, trimming stones for graveyards. With the aid of three crowbars, we moved the first stone, and found under it a silver coin similar to the one previously picked up; under the second stone we found another coin similar to the previous two. I then called my wife and niece to assist me in my discovery. On their coming up, we removed the third stone, and found a part of a ring—say a garnet set in gold, and some crumbs of gold; under the fourth stone we found a gold olive leaf, a terra-cotta seal, and some crumbs of gold. We searched amongst the rubbish for more, but without success, so went to lunch.

Clarke eventually ended up with a haul of six tetradrachms (silver coins worth four drachms) of Orophernes, as fresh as the day they were struck, which had lain undisturbed under the base of the statue of Athena for a little over 2,000 years. (He later presented the finest of the coins—illustrated here, Figure 16—to the British Museum.) This extraordinary find leaves us with a tantalizing puzzle. Did Orophernes perhaps pay for a new cult-statue of Athena, and inter a handful of his own coins as a kind of 'ritual deposit' in the earth beneath the base of the new statue? Or might the Prieneans have surreptitiously creamed off a few coins from Orophernes' 400 talents, and squirrelled them away in a safe place for a rainy day?

Figure 16 Tetradrachm of Orophernes, discovered by A. C. Clarke in 1870.

Life in the City

For the Greek cities of Asia Minor, the 'Classical' period of the fifth and fourth centuries BC had meant political subjection to Achaemenid Persia or imperial Athens; the coming of Roman rule after 133 BC brought crippling levels of taxation and the rapid hollowing-out of civic institutions. By comparison, the Hellenistic period was something of a golden age for the Greeks of Asia Minor. Some historians have dismissed the 'autonomy and freedom' bestowed by Hellenistic kings on cities such as Priene as little more than empty slogans, designed to paper over the reality of Macedonian domination. At least in the case of Priene, this is quite wrong. The kings did not interfere with Priene's internal affairs. The Prieneans struck their own silver and bronze coinage, and the city's democratic assembly passed decrees and had them inscribed on stone with impressive assiduity.

So far as we know, the Prieneans paid no tax or tribute to any Hellenistic monarch, and even in foreign policy they retained a large measure of independence (the city fought several significant wars with its neighbours in the third and second centuries BC).

Hellenistic Priene was governed as a democracy, with an assembly of all adult male citizens—the *dēmos* or 'people'—acting as the supreme decision-making body. Specialized boards of officials (grain-commissioners, guardians of law, religious officials) were appointed by the assembly, usually for a year at a time, and were accountable to the people for their actions and expenditure. In practice, most of these offices would always have been filled by the wealthiest citizens of Priene: indeed, certain religious offices, such as the priesthoods of Dionysus Phleus, the Phrygian Mother and of Poseidon Heliconius, were openly sold for life to the highest bidder.

It is hard to say how often the democratic assembly actually met. Of the twenty-five surviving decrees of Hellenistic Priene which are dated by the month, no fewer than eighteen were passed at assembly meetings held in the month Metageitnion (August/September). In nine of those eighteen cases the day of the month is also specified, and the fifth day of Metageitnion turns out to have been particularly popular (five out of nine cases). In a couple of surviving decrees, this annual meeting in early Metageitnion is described as the 'election meeting' (*archairēsiai*), the meeting at which the civic magistrates for the following year were appointed. Clearly this summer 'election meeting' rattled through a lot of business—not just elections—at high speed; whether the assembly met regularly throughout the rest of the year is less obvious. Nor do we know how many citizens regularly attended the assembly at Priene. At the nearby cities of Magnesia on the Maeander and Colophon, where voting figures are occasionally recorded, the numbers of citizens voting in the assembly ranged between 2,113 and 4,678 (Magnesia, a slightly larger place than Priene) and 903 and 1,342 (Colophon, perhaps a little smaller).

Priene did not impose direct income taxes on its citizens. Instead, many of the city's expenses were met by the assignment of specific 'liturgies' (compulsory financial contributions) to individual wealthy Prieneans. When the Prieneans put the civic priesthood of Dionysus Phleus up for auction around 130 BC, one of the terms of sale was that the successful purchaser would be exempted from a whole series of civic liturgies (the organization of torch-races and athletic contests, the raising of horses, the funding of sacred embassies, the administration of the gymnasium), on condition that he paid more than 6,000 drachms for the priesthood.

The sons of Prienean citizens were divided into three age-classes, *paides* ('boys', aged between about twelve and eighteen), *ephēboi* ('adolescents', around eighteen to twenty) and *neoi* ('young men', around twenty to thirty). Members of all three age-classes were educated at the city's two lavish gymnasia, institutions dedicated to the physical, intellectual, and cultural training of Prienean youth. A series of honorific decrees of the early first century BC for a wealthy Prienean citizen called Zosimus gives us some sense of the education on offer at Priene. Zosimus personally presided over a set of oral examinations for the city's *paides*, donating splendid

Figure 17 The rock of Teloneia, seen from the sanctuary of Athena.

the daily rounds in person (first on his own, later along with his son) to see to the security of the guard-post; he was attentive to the members of his garrison, not least in making sure that all receive equal treatment, and that all the affairs of the rock be conducted smoothly and without disputes; and he acted throughout his term of office with honesty and justice, exhorting his men to guard the rock with the greatest care, bearing in mind that there is nothing more important for Greek men than freedom.

The decree for Helicon was voted not by the Prienean assembly, but by the young men of the garrison, who—remarkably—sent two of their number as 'ambassadors' to the town of Priene (as if to a foreign city) to ask that the honours for Helicon be inscribed on stone. The garrison clearly saw itself as a kind of city-within-the-city, with its own decision-making body and distinct military ethos.

We know much less about the intimate life of the Prienean household. Most private houses at Priene were laid out on a uniform plan, with a single unobtrusive street-entrance leading to a small interior courtyard. The courtyard generally had a modest open portico on the north side, acting as a sun-trap, with two living-rooms and a men's dining room ('*andrōn*') grouped around it. There appears to have been a rigid separation of male and female domestic space, with the women's quarters located on an upper floor above the portico. In the course of the Hellenistic period, some of the wealthier citizens of Priene became dissatisfied with these tidy little housing units, and knocked through the party walls into neighbouring houses to form larger composite dwellings. The biggest surviving house in Priene ('House 33', a stone's throw from the sanctuary of Athena) was created around 100 BC by combining two existing houses into a single sprawling complex, laid out around a lavish peristyle courtyard of a type unknown in early Hellenistic Priene. It is even conceivable that the house's owner was influenced by the great Italian dwellings of contemporary Roman aristocrats.

From Apellis to Moschion

The late Hellenistic redesign of House 33 fits neatly into a broader pattern of social change at Priene. Although early Hellenistic Priene was no egalitarian paradise, it was a place where private wealth was relatively unobtrusive. The physical fabric of the city, its government and civic institutions, and the language of Prienean public documents all reflected a collectivist citizen ideology. Since office-holders were expected to meet the expenses of their post from their own pockets, it was usually the richer citizens who were elected to the main civic offices. But these men were in no sense masters of their city. In the late fourth and third centuries BC, when Priene honoured its wealthy citizens for their patriotism and lavish expenditure, they were honoured purely and solely in their capacity as elected office-holders. Here, for example, are the first few lines of a typical honorific decree of the late fourth century BC, for a wealthy Prienean called Apellis:

> Having been elected as Secretary (*grammateus*) by the *dēmos*, he has provided his services in a fair-minded and just manner to each of the citizens, in law-suits, in his custody and oversight of public documents, and in all his other duties to the city; and in legal disputes involving the entire city, he has continually proved to be capable and earnest, making it his first priority to be seen to be acting justly. And he has now come before the assembly and explained that he has held public office for twenty years in all, for fourteen of which he has performed the liturgy [compulsory public service] of Secretary to the generals at his own expense, and that he has absolved the *dēmos* from payment of the stipend set aside by law for the Secretary to the guardians of law and the office-holders, and that during this time he has been crowned on four occasions by the *dēmos*, and he now requests that he be released from the office of Secretary and permitted to retire from public affairs.

Apellis was obviously a very rich man. But his involvement in civic affairs was always and only as an elected holder of public office: we know from another document that he also acted as garrison-commander on Teloneia at some point during his career. The city conferred honours on him as an exemplary democratic official, not as a powerful local 'big man' or patron.

In the second and first centuries BC, this changed. Here are the first few lines of a typical honorific decree of the late second century BC, for a rich citizen called Moschion:

> Having shown himself to be a fine and good man from his earliest youth, living in piety towards the gods, and with devotion towards his parents, his household kinsmen and companions, and all the rest of the citizens, he has conducted himself towards his homeland in a spirit of justice and ambition, worthy of the virtue and fame of his ancestors. Throughout his entire life, he has received abundant proofs of the favour of the gods towards him, and of the goodwill of his fellow-citizens and the other residents of the city, arising from his most splendid deeds...

We are instantly transported into a very different political climate. Now a rich man is worthy of honour not just for his tenure of democratic offices, but for his hereditary 'virtue and fame', and his personal splendour in the eyes of the gods and his adoring fellow-citizens. As the account of Moschion's career unfolds—383 lines of it, all written in the same glutinous prose-style—it gradually becomes clear that he is no mere office-holder. Again and again, he offers cash loans and gifts to the city on his own account, provides cut-price grain from his estates in times of famine, and bestows lavish free banquets and distributions of wine and bread on the citizen body. When the money for a new gymnasium which had been promised by an unnamed Hellenistic king (probably Attalus III, reigned 138–133 BC) fails to arrive due to the extinction of the royal line, Moschion steps in and provides the funds himself.

It is hard to say whether Moschion was actually richer than Apellis (I suspect that he was), but he certainly occupied a completely different place in the civic life of Priene. As the French scholar Philippe Gauthier has put it, reflecting on the careers of Moschion and his contemporaries:

> The great benefactors [of the later Hellenistic period] are no longer just generals, ambassadors, or officials, who are appointed, instructed, and finally honoured for their actions by the people... At one and the same time the 'saviours' of their homeland at times of crisis, and its benefactors on a day-to-day basis, they come to look less and less like the political actors whom their communities honoured in the early Hellenistic period. They gradually start to become the 'patrons' of their city.

This change can be seen everywhere in the physical fabric of the city, not just in the emergence of big mansions like House 33. In the *agora* of Priene, the city's main public space, honorific statues for great civic benefactors sprouted like weeds along the main thoroughfare. At what must have been one of the busiest street-corners of Priene, where a broad flight of stairs leads up from the *agora* to the sanctuary of Athena, two statues of the same man (a certain Apollodorus) were erected right in front of the steps, forcing any Prienean entering or leaving the *agora* to skirt around their plinths. The back wall of the stoa on the north side of the *agora*—no doubt the most welcoming of all Prienean public spaces during the hot Mediterranean summer—was covered with endless inscriptions hymning the virtues of Moschion and men like him.

Perhaps most striking of all, we find the wives and daughters of the very rich starting to play a prominent role in public life. An inscription of the first century BC records the construction of an aqueduct and water-distribution system by a female benefactor (her name is not preserved), described as the first woman to hold the major Prienean civic office of 'wreath-bearer' (*stephanēphoros*). To our modern sensibilities, the holding of public office by a woman seems like a most welcome and enlightened development. But in the context of ancient Greek civic politics— traditionally the preserve of male citizens only—it in fact reflects the final capture of Prienean democracy by the city's aristocratic class. The dominance of the great benefactors was now so complete that even their female relatives could be parachuted into civic offices. By the first century BC, the civic institutions of Priene were entirely in the hands of a few noble families.

The later history of Priene is largely a blank. The population of the city seems already to have been in decline in the late second century BC, when a fire swept through the whole western residential district; this part of the town was never subsequently rebuilt. The city's rich documentary record comes to an abrupt halt in the mid-first century BC, and after a modest revival under Augustus (27 BC–AD 14), the town became a sleepy backwater in the Roman Imperial period.

In this book, we have seen something of the staggering variety and complexity of the Hellenistic civilization that emerged out of the conquests of Alexander of Macedon: a world blazing with light and life, from the frontier Greek settlements of central Asia to the luxurious villas of central Italy, and from the scientific powerhouse of Ptolemaic Alexandria to the bustling small towns of Asia Minor. No single town or city could possibly encapsulate the entire history of the Greek-speaking world in the three centuries from the death of Alexander to the accession of Augustus. This chapter could equally well have focussed on Hellenistic Athens, Jerusalem, Philadelphia in Egypt, or the Attalid capital of Pergamon in north-west Asia Minor, all of them at least as richly documented as Hellenistic Priene. But Priene is a fine enough vantage point from which to look out across the vast expanses of the Hellenistic world—that brief and wonderful moment in human history when, as William Tarn once remarked, the Greek language 'might take a man from Marseilles to India, from the Caspian to the Cataracts'.

TIMELINE

All dates are BC.

336	Death of Philip II of Macedon; accession of Alexander III ('the Great')
334	Macedonian invasion of Asia
332	Foundation of Alexandria
331	Battle of Gaugamela; defeat of Darius III of Persia
327–325	Alexander campaigns in India
323	Death of Alexander the Great; Lysimachus and Ptolemy satraps of Thrace and Egypt
320	Conference of Triparadeisus; Seleucus satrap of Babylon
317	Death of Philip III Arrhidaeus
310	Death of Alexander IV; end of Argead monarchy of Macedon
307	Capture of Athens by Demetrius the Besieger
306	Antigonus the One-Eyed and Demetrius the Besieger proclaimed as kings
305	Ptolemy I Soter proclaimed as king in Egypt
305–304	Siege of Rhodes by Demetrius the Besieger

301	Battle of Ipsus; death of Antigonus the One-Eyed
300–290	Clearchus of Soli visits Aï Khanoum
297	Death of Cassander in Macedon
294–288	Demetrius the Besieger rules in Macedon
282	Death of Ptolemy I Soter of Egypt
281	Battle of Corupedium; death of Lysimachus; death of Seleucus I Nicator
280–278	Galatian invasion of mainland Greece
280–275	Pyrrhus of Epirus campaigns in Italy and Sicily
276	Antigonus II Gonatas recovers Macedon
262	(?) Battle of Cos; Antigonid dominance in the Aegean
246	Death of Ptolemy II Philadelphus of Egypt; Ptolemy III Euergetes campaigns in Asia
245	Bactria revolts from Seleucids
238	(?) Attalus I of Pergamon proclaimed as king
220–216	Polybius' *symplokē*; Rome enters the Greek East
214–205	First Macedonian War
212–196	Antiochus III reconquers Iran and Asia Minor
201	Rome defeats Hannibal in Second Punic War
200–197	Second Macedonian War; Flamininus defeats Philip V at Kynoskephalai
196	Flamininus proclaims freedom of the Greeks at Corinth
190	Battle of Magnesia
188	Treaty of Apamea; Seleucids expelled from Asia Minor
188–133	Attalid rule in Asia Minor
171–168	Third Macedonian War
170–168	Campaigns of Antiochus IV in Egypt

168	Battle of Pydna; end of Antigonid monarchy
167–160	Maccabean revolt against Seleucids in Judaea
146	Achaean War; sack of Corinth; establishment of Roman province of Macedonia
145	(?) Sack of Aï Khanoum
144	Ptolemy VIII expels intellectuals from Egypt
133	Death of Attalus III; end of Attalid monarchy
129	Establishment of Roman province of Asia
120–115	Eudoxus' discovery of the sea-route to India
89–63	Mithradatic Wars between Rome and Mithradates VI of Pontus
64	End of Seleucid monarchy; establishment of Roman province of Syria
31	Battle of Actium
30	Death of Cleopatra VII; Roman conquest of Egypt

FURTHER READING

CHAPTER 1: THE IDEA OF THE HELLENISTIC

The travels of Clearchus of Soli were first reconstructed by the French scholar Louis Robert, the greatest modern historian of antiquity; Robert's 'De Delphes à l'Oxus: inscriptions grecques nouvelles de la Bactriane', *CRAI* (1968), 416–57, remains perhaps the single most inspiring article ever written on the Hellenistic Age. Johann Gustav Droysen's conception of the 'Hellenistic' is discussed by Arnaldo Momigliano, 'J. G. Droysen between Greeks and Jews', *History and Theory* 9/2 (1970), 139–53, reprinted in *A. D. Momigliano: Studies on Modern Scholarship* (Berkeley and Los Angeles: University of California Press, 1994), 147–61. The most accessible (and entertaining) narrative sources for the period are Plutarch's biographies of Hellenistic rulers, translated in the Oxford World's Classics series by Robin Waterfield, *Plutarch: Hellenistic Lives* (Oxford: Oxford University Press, 2016). The rich Egyptian papyrological documentation is brought to life by Naphtali Lewis, *Greeks in Ptolemaic Egypt* (Oxford: Clarendon Press, 1986). A good selection of Hellenistic inscriptions in translation can be found in Michel Austin's *The Hellenistic World from Alexander to the Roman Conquest*, second edition (Cambridge: Cambridge University Press, 2006). I provide an overview of the coinages of the Hellenistic world in my own *The Hellenistic World: Using Coins as Sources* (Cambridge: Cambridge University Press, 2015).

CHAPTER 2: FROM ALEXANDER TO AUGUSTUS

Frank Walbank's *The Hellenistic World* (London: Fontana, 1981; revised edition, 1992) is a reliable and readable guide to Hellenistic history, now supplemented by the essays collected in Andrew Erskine (ed.), *A Companion to the Hellenistic World* (Malden, MA: Blackwell, 2003). Graham Shipley's *The Greek World After Alexander, 323–30 BC* (London and New York: Routledge, 2000) is also recommended. The conquest of Asia by Alexander of Macedon (334–323 BC) comes to life in the hands of Pierre Briant, *Alexander the Great and his Empire: A Short Introduction* (Princeton: Princeton University Press, 2010). The most insightful treatment of Alexander's early successors is Mary Renault's novel *Funeral Games* (London: John Murray, 1981). The Seleucid kingdom is the subject of a fine recent monograph by Paul Kosmin, *The Land of the Elephant Kings* (Cambridge, MA: Harvard University Press, 2014), while the Ptolemaic dynasty of Egypt is best approached through Günther Hölbl, *A History of the Ptolemaic Empire* (London and New York: Routledge, 2001). The Adulis inscription of Ptolemy III is discussed in Glen Bowersock's *The Throne of Adulis* (Oxford: Oxford University

Press, 2013). The poems of C. P. Cavafy—an excellent introduction to Hellenistic culture—are translated into English in the Oxford World's Classics series by Evangelos Sachperoglou, *C. P. Cavafy: The Collected Poems* (Oxford: Oxford University Press, 2008). The rise of Rome is unflinchingly narrated in the collected essays of Peter Derow, *Rome, Polybius, & the East* (Oxford: Oxford University Press, 2014).

CHAPTER 3: DEMETRIUS THE BESIEGER AND HELLENISTIC KINGSHIP

The centrality of military conquest to Hellenistic royal ideology is emphasized by Michel Austin, 'Hellenistic Kings, war and the economy', *Classical Quarterly* 36 (1986) 450–66. The classic analysis of Hellenistic royal images, in sculpture and on coins, is R. R. R. Smith, *Hellenistic Royal Portraits* (Oxford: Clarendon Press, 1988). For the Hellenistic king at war, consult Angelos Chaniotis, *War in the Hellenistic World* (Oxford: Blackwell, 2005). The most helpful starting point for Hellenistic ruler-worship is Simon Price's *Rituals and Power: The Roman Imperial Cult in Asia Minor* (Cambridge: Cambridge University Press, 1986). The inscription recording the establishment of a Seleucid ruler-cult at Aegae can be found in *Supplementum Epigraphicum Graecum* 59 (2009), 1406.

CHAPTER 4: ERATOSTHENES AND THE SYSTEM OF THE WORLD

General accounts of science and scholarship in Hellenistic Alexandria can be found in R. Pfeiffer, *History of Classical Scholarship from the Beginnings to the End of the Hellenistic Age* (Oxford: Clarendon Press, 1968) and P. M. Fraser, *Ptolemaic Alexandria* (Oxford: Clarendon Press, 1972). The best short account of the Alexandrian Library is that of R. S. Bagnall, 'Alexandria: Library of Dreams', *Proceedings of the American Philosophical Society,* 146/4 (2002), 348–62. The surviving fragments of Eratosthenes' *Geography* are translated and discussed by D. Roller, *Eratosthenes' Geography* (Princeton and Oxford: Princeton University Press, 2009). J. P. Oleson (ed.), *The Oxford Handbook of Engineering and Technology in the Classical World* (Oxford: Oxford University Press, 2008) provides an excellent introduction to Greek and Roman technology, in which Hellenistic innovations play a major role; a selection of translated texts can be found in G. L. Irby-Massie and P. T. Keyser, *Greek Science of the Hellenistic Era: A Sourcebook* (London and New York: Routledge, 2003). R. Netz, *Ludic Proof: Greek Mathematics and the Alexandrian Aesthetic* (Cambridge: Cambridge University Press, 2009) is a lively study of the 'interface' between Hellenistic mathematics and poetry. Stoic and Epicurean philosophy receive a sympathetic hearing from M. C. Nussbaum, *The Therapy of Desire: Theory and Practice in Hellenistic Ethics* (Princeton: Princeton University Press, 1994).

CHAPTER 5: ENCOUNTERS

There are good photographs of Aï Khanoum and its major artefacts in the British Museum exhibition catalogue *Afghanistan: Crossroads of the Ancient World* (London: British Museum Press, 2011); the best introduction to the history of the site is now Rachel Mairs, *The Hellenistic Far East* (Oakland, CA: University of California Press, 2014). Iromois' dedication to the Oxus can be found in Georges Rougemont, *Inscriptions grecques d'Iran et d'Asie centrale* (London: SOAS, 2012), 96 bis. The Greek historian Arrian describes Nearchus' exploration of the northern shores of the Indian Ocean in his *Indica*, translated in the Oxford World's Classics series by Martin Hammond, *Arrian: Alexander the Great, the Anabasis and the Indica* (Oxford: Oxford University Press, 2013). Posidonius' account of the travels of Eudoxus of Cyzicus is preserved in Strabo's *Geography* (2.3.4), translated for the Loeb Classical Library by H. L. Jones, *Strabo: Geography, Books 1–2* (Cambridge, Mass.: Harvard University Press, 1917). The decree for Protogenes of Olbia is translated by Michel Austin, *The Hellenistic World from Alexander to the Roman Conquest*, second edition (Cambridge: Cambridge University Press, 2006), no. 115. For the Villa of the Papyri, see Carol C. Mattusch, *The Villa dei Papiri at Herculaneum: Life and Afterlife of a Sculpture Collection* (Los Angeles: The J. Paul Getty Museum, 2005), and David Sider, *The Library of the Villa dei Papiri at Herculaneum* (Los Angeles: The J. Paul Getty Museum, 2005).

CHAPTER 6: PRIENE

The best short introduction to Priene in English is Frank Rumscheid's well-illustrated guidebook, *Priene: A Guide to the 'Pompeii of Asia Minor'* (Istanbul: Ege Yayınları, 1998). The wider geographic context of the city's history is sketched in my own *The Maeander Valley: A Historical Geography from Antiquity to Byzantium* (Cambridge: Cambridge University Press, 2011). All of the Greek inscriptions discussed in this chapter are published with German translations in W. Blümel and R. Merkelbach, *Die Inschriften von Priene* (Bonn: Habelt, 2014); the decrees honouring Sotas and conferring ruler-cult on Lysimachus are translated into English by Stanley M. Burstein, *The Hellenistic Age from the Battle of Ipsos to the Death of Cleopatra VII* (Cambridge: Cambridge University Press, 1985), nos. 10 and 17. Alexander's edict to Priene is discussed by Susan Sherwin-White, 'Ancient Archives: the Edict of Alexander to Priene, a Reappraisal,' *JHS* 105 (1985), 69–89, and in my own 'Alexander, Priene, and Naulochon', in P. Martzavou and N. Papazarkadas (eds), *Epigraphical Approaches to the Post-Classical Polis* (Oxford: Oxford University Press, 2013), 23–36. Clarke's day-trip to Priene in 1870 is recounted by C. T. Newton, 'On an Inedited Tetradrachm of Orophernes II', *Numismatic Chronicle* n.s. xi (1871), 19–27. John Ma discusses the 'statue habit' at Priene, and the changes that it brought to the city's public spaces, in his magnificent *Statues and Cities: Honorific Portraits and Civic Identity in the*

Hellenistic World (Oxford: Oxford University Press, 2013). The rise of the great civic benefactors of the later Hellenistic period is traced by Philippe Gauthier, *Les cités grecques et leurs bienfaiteurs* (Athens and Paris: de Boccard, 1985).

PUBLISHER'S ACKNOWLEDGEMENTS

We are grateful for permission to include the following copyright material in this book:

'The Battle of Magnesia' from *Cavafy: Collected Poems, Oxford World Classics* translated by Evangelos Sachperoglou (2007) by kind permission of Oxford University Press.

The publisher and author have made every effort to trace and contact all copyright holders before publication. If notified, the publisher will be pleased to rectify any errors or omissions at the earliest opportunity.

INDEX

Index

Index